Letters from Sawdust

Sawdust

Letters from Sawdust

by

Isabelle H. Klein

with illustrations by
WILLIAM E. SCHEELE

The Cobham and Hatherton Press
Cleveland, Ohio
1988

LETTERS FROM SAWDUST
Copyright © 1988 by Isabelle H. Klein
First Edition
Book design by Roderick Boyd Porter
Illustrations by William E. Scheele

Library of Congress Cataloging-in-Publication Data
Klein, Isabelle H.
    Letters from Sawdust.
    1. Natural history — Ohio — Ashtabula County.
I. Title.
QH105.O3K55   1988   508.771'34   87-30013
ISBN 0-944125-04-2

DEDICATED TO DICK, RICK, AND MILCEY
AND ALL MY FRIENDS
WHO SHARED THE HAPPY TIMES
AND EXCITING DISCOVERIES
AT SAWDUST TRACT

CONTENTS

3	Letter One: Winter 1969
9	Letter Two: Spring 1970
15	Letter Three: Summer 1970
21	Letter Four: Fall 1970
27	Letter Five: Spring 1971
33	Letter Six: Summer 1971
39	Letter Seven: Fall 1971
45	Letter Eight: Winter 1971
51	Letter Nine: Spring 1972
57	Letter Ten: Summer 1972
65	Letter Eleven: Fall 1972
71	Letter Twelve: Winter 1972
77	Letter Thirteen: Spring 1973
83	Letter Fourteen: Summer 1973
89	Letter Fifteen: Fall 1973
95	Letter Sixteen: Winter 1973
101	Letter Seventeen: Fall 1974
107	Letter Eighteen: Winter 1974
113	Letter Nineteen: Spring 1975
119	Letter Twenty: Summer 1975

Illustrations

Frontispiece	Sawdust
2	Tufted titmouse
8	Spotted salamander
14	Snapping turtle
19	Bluebird
20	Coneheaded grasshopper
25	Least shrew
26	Red-shouldered hawk
31	Wood frog
32	Male bobolink
32	Jewel weed (Touch-me-not)
44	Great-horned owl
50	American toad
55	Green heron
56	Rabbit and young
63	Cottontail rabbit
64	Chicory
70	Wild grape
75	Ichneuman fly
76	Four spring buds
81	Flowers of the shadbush
82	Hummingbird nest
87	Branch
88	Red squirrel
93	Maple-leaved viburnum
94	Partridge berry
99	Katydids
100	Male cricket
106	Katydid and beaver
111	Northern shrike
112	Beaver
118	White-footed mouse

Foreword

MORE THAN A DECADE AGO, a group of us were circled about a dying fire in our woodland, Sawdust Tract, listening to the katydids and cherishing the sight of a rising full moon. It was then that Joann Scheele, editor of *The Explorer,* turned to me and quietly asked if I would consider sharing my experiences and observations at Sawdust with her readers. The marshmallow I was toasting sputtered, as did a sudden concern: would I be able to clearly interpret the unfolding drama I experienced each day at Sawdust? I told her I would love to try.

The following years were special ones, as I walked those trails. I felt perhaps hundreds of pairs of eyes were viewing each occurrence with me, rather than I alone being permitted to see it all.

And now those letters have been gathered together and republished with exquisite drawings done by William E. Scheele. It is so appropriate that he is the artist illustrating them, since the Sawdust Letters would not have been written had it not been for Bill and his wife Joann. (William E. Scheele was the director of the Cleveland Museum of Natural History, which published *The Explorer.*) I am deeply indebted to them both!

Sawdust Tract is still there, but I am not. I know that the continuity nurtured by Nature guarantees that most of what I saw and described is there yet, for other generations to observe. My home now is an old homesteader's log cabin in one of Wyoming's Wind River Mountain valleys. As any other naturalist would do, I am diligently attempting to acquaint myself with this most challenging land. But I miss the reassurance of the familiar and, as I have long known, there is no place that I shall ever love more than our Sawdust Tract.

Isabelle H. Klein
July 11, 1987
Pavillion, Wyoming

In Ashtabula County, Ohio, there is a place known as Sawdust. It includes more than five hundred acres of cut-over woods and tired farm land that is officially designated the Sawdust Tract Biological Survey Area. Here Richard and Isabelle Klein and their children lived and worked together to study and document the inter-relationship of the plants and animals that live there. As this family of naturalists was separated for school terms or summer jobs from time to time, letters flew back and forth as in all families. The letters from Sawdust differ from most exchanges because the close personal bond with the land comes through. The slowly disappearing sawdust piles and swift-growing saplings have provided a revelation of plant succession and wildlife populations that have not been previously studied. Letters from Sawdust *are gleaned from letters written during a period of several years; the observations reveal an understanding and feeling for the natural world that is a rare thing today.*

Tufted titmouse

Letter One: *Winter 1969*

December 1st. Several soft, warm, gentle days have beguiled all of Sawdust; though it is December, squat golden yard-dandelions bloom flat against their vitamin-packed, dark green leaves, while around our pond silvery gray pussywillows push aside their maroon caps and honeybees drink along the moist matted edge. Robins, still feeding on the wild grapes, sing short, subdued, tender, tentative songs. As I pick a few short-stemmed deep blue violets, I cannot help but think everything is in order except the weather.

Not until it is dark do I manage to slip back to the woods, silvered by moonlight. The woodland at night is intriguing for so often I hear a scream or cry that I am unable to identify; then there are things like tiny, glowing spider eyes or chittering flying squirrels that land so silently.

Tonight, the trees stand bare shoulder to shoulder against the long moonlit sky. Too soon this will become a silent battleground with only the most instinctive or lucky animal surviving the icy clutch of weather, jaw, or talon.

A chipping cardinal flusters out of a grapevine thicket I pass too closely. Late today we had an interesting return of a banded male cardinal. Two years ago we trapped and tagged this bird; at that time he was beginning to lose his head feathers. Within twelve weeks he was bare-headed, frequently tucking his gray skull with its bulging bluish eye sockets beneath his wing. Blizzards, below-zero weather — each day I thought would surely be his last. So did a neighbor two-thirds of a mile away for he divided his feeding periods between her supply of sunflower seeds and ours. With the coming of warm weather, neither of us saw that banded, bald cardinal again. But today he was retrapped and sported as beautiful a head of crimson feathers as any. I dialed my neighbor.

Half a mile later, prowling up a small rise, I marvel once more over our largest standing chestnut tree, dead probably for thirty or forty years, seen many times by day, never before by bright night. It is so easy to dream by moonbeams; standing there

3

I see the ghosts of those who might have passed that tree since possibly a gray squirrel first patted the chestnut into the ground: elk, wolves, otter, bison, mountain lions, bobcats, passenger pigeons, Indians or early settlers gathering moss with which to stuff a wild turkey. A bone-whitened giant of a tree, a lonely ultimate reminder of what was. Still, though, part of the woodland, for birds nest in its hollowed branches and the largest black rat snake I have ever seen on Sawdust Tract slowly disappeared into its center one day. The wild night that it splits and crashes to the ground will begin a whole new chapter as the chestnut tree hosts a different kind of life and it is one with the soil. I return home, too.

* * *

December 15th. Walking across a browned, stiffened, weedy field today made me happy we had allowed the goldenrod, asters, milkweed, sedges, sumac, and willows to have their way.

Tree sparrows flew up while a downy woodpecker remained, too preoccupied chipping open a tawny rounded gall on a Canada goldenrod stem, hoping to find a fat pale-yellow larva. How do woodpeckers know that there is a bit of live food inside that swollen goldenrod stem? I count thirty-one galls that have been laid bare; thirty-one flies *(Eurosta solidaginis)* won't be flying over a field next summer. Such incredible flies, though! A single egg is deposited on the goldenrod, hatches, and the tiny larva bores into the growing stem and somehow induces the plant then to manufacture its home — a waterproof, insulated, nutritious ball about the size of a hickory nut. Molecular biologists would know what manner of substance they use to initiate and stimulate such cellular changes; I just have to be content to know that it happens.

A milkweed pod, split lengthwise but still cradling its delicate cargo of three hundred seeds, attracts me. Flattened, brown seeds, each one attached to a circled tuft of hundreds of long white hairs. Botanists refer to this tuft as a coma, a dull name for something so exquisitely fashioned, hairs that can buoyantly float the tiny seed far from this field, hairs as soft as those of a wee infant with the pure whiteness of truth that comes with age. They will surely soon drift away in time on their own, but who is able to resist shaking the stalk, blowing a bit? I want to be there to see the billowing, silken parachutes caught up by the wind; some reach so high I can scarcely make them out against the blue sky, others soon come to rest nearby — all of them carrying the most precious gift of all — Life. I see a new plant growing somewhere; fragrant, rounded clusters of dustyrose flowers hanging heavy with nectar, honey bees, harlequin caterpillars, or a monarch butterfly poised above, about to trust that plant with its egg and larva.

I watched a tufted titmouse on the way home furiously pounding a seed clutched between his toes; I wonder if he ever misses with that hammer?

* * *

December 24th. Half a mile from the house, half a mile from anyone's house, I stand in our quiet valley, anticipating in a childlike way some very special Christmas Eve treat: the sight of a red fox, a winter wren or white-winged crossbills twisting the hemlock cones. There is nothing; it is a silent world and I am alone. Suddenly, I realize that evanescent gifts are being heaped upon the earth, on the stumps, old bird nests, bracken mushrooms, on rocks, branches, and me. Absolutely *perfect* snowflakes! Only nature can bestow that which man cannot improve.

* * *

January 1st. May the priceless chain of Nature's Checks and Balances help shield all through the coming year.

* * *

January 18th. Below zero outside, winds whipping the meadow drifts into snowy dunes. The whole farmyard world sounds cold, but when I flick on the kitchen light a now familiar little song greets me. My way of prolonging a season perhaps, but a grasshopper does make a cheerful addition to my winter kitchen. Chief Green Grass Hopper (named for one of the Indian chiefs who long ago sold the Western Reserve lands to Moses Cleaveland) has sung his way into our hearts. One rondo for the daytime, a different one by night. Collected late last September, he is no longer a bright green meadow grasshopper. He has darkened, lost an antenna, frayed in parts, I would say. But still he sings; Zip-zip-zip-zeeeeee. The secret to keeping him alive, I believe, is a dry home. Each day I hop him into a clean jelly glass with but a single piece of green lettuce. His technical name is *Orchelimum vulgare*.

* * *

February 4th. The storm of the crooked icicles is past; curious to see what is about now, I tie on my snowshoes and print my way down the trail to the valley. While I plod, our St. Bernard bounds — great joyous leaps; but she breaks through, I do not. Neither do the ruffed grouse, for they now have short, grayish, flat projections rimming their toes.

Everywhere there are tracks, too crisscrossed always to properly unravel. The red fox are running in pairs now; hope a pair returns to the den nearest the house, for there they won't be smoked, blasted, or dug out. The fox must be smart, indeed — instinctively brilliant to survive the vindictiveness with which it is pursued three hundred and sixty-five days a year in Ohio. No longer just a fine winter sport with excited full-crying hounds, it has turned into an electronic, mechanized battle. Walkie-talkies, airplanes, snowmobiles, tape recorders broadcasting the squeals of dying rabbits or lovesick vixens; all are used. Each year, though, we still have fox.

The tiny embroidered tracks of a shrew come out of a snowy hole, preceded by a frightened white-footed mouse jumping into the great snowy beyond. The shrew does not follow very far. Neatly lying in the snow by the entrance of another small hole there are three empty, but unbroken, shells of the land snail, *Triodopsis tridentata*.

From the sound ahead, a pileated woodpecker must be piling up the wood chips. He was gone before I could see him; however, I must have interrupted a fine meal, for he had knocked his way into a cluster of large carpenter ants — a crystallized, frosty mass of fat abdomens and shiny black heads, just awaiting spring to thaw. The insects that live in rotten wood and beneath bark throughout the winter somehow must manufacture a fancy type of anti-freeze for themselves.

A mink track crosses the trail, disappears into a whitened grapevine jungle, reappears, and continues on. I follow. A frolicsome, lighthearted hunter he is though, for at one place he quickened his pace and then tobogganed down a short hillside. Wish I had been there to watch. Fox squirrel tracks all head toward the farmyard, for the squirrels have learned that golden cobs are strung up, kernels of past work and sunshine.

The valley, no limit to beauty here, undefaced, glorious. No breeze to shuffle the mounds of snow from the hemlock branches but perhaps a landing bluejay will. A thousand frozen topaz tears, caught trickling down the shaley banks; tears, that in the springtime will water the smaller enchanter's nightshade *(C. alpina)*, or the hobblebush *(V. alnifolium)*, and fly honeysuckle *(L. canadensis)* shrubs clinging so precariously to the steep-sided cold bank.

The St. Bernard and I rest here, sharing apples and a lump of maple sugar before we complete the loop. I leave a handful of sunflower seeds and bits of apple on a whisked-off stump; my atonement for shattering the peacefulness of the valley.

Spotted salamander

LETTER TWO: *Spring 1970*

IF NATURE RATIONS ANYTHING, it is perfect springtime days — so many to each spring of one's life, impossible to hoard, and, with the crush of living, impossible sometimes to savor. This one opened with the distribution of sugar spikes and heavy galvanized sap pails. To stand in the sugarbush and hear the plunking of sap drops, each tap with its own tempo and sound, was to hear the impatient finale of winter. No matter that snow still blanketed the ground; the sun was warm, crows called, chickadees whistled "so-o-o sweee-et," columns of midges danced up and down like so many tiny yo-yos over a patch of bare earth, and brown, delicate lacewings fluttered into the sap buckets.

Every time I see a brown lacewing (a neuropteran related to the Dobson fly) I think of its tiny larval form that I found by accident one fall. I collected it, believing it to be a cluster of minute land snail shells and not until I had it focused beneath the microscope lens did I realize it was an insect which had concealed its body by plastering snail shells on its back. That little trash beater (only one-fifth of an inch) had gathered together at least five species of snails, none of them more than two millimeters long or wide, and had the load all held together with sticky cobwebby strands supported by whorled sets of bristles on each side of its back. Naturally, I was curious to watch how he operated, so I placed a live white carychium snail near him. With jaws resembling ice tongs, he clasped the tiny shell and skillfully worked it into the pile on his back. Those jaw pincers, constantly opening and closing, were like those of the male hellgrammite (the larva of the Dobson fly and well known to fishermen as terrific bass bait). For days I watched that little fellow, constantly wondering when and how such a particular behavior pattern had evolved. There are an estimated twenty thousand species of insects found in this region and I would wager that there are twenty thousand equally fascinating adaptions, many not yet known or fully understood.

The swelling buds concluded the maple syrup operation but

left me free to walk the trails again. While I roamed, Dick was visited daily in his barn workshop by one of the rarest mammals in Ohio, the shorttail weasel. The lithe, sleek animal with its four white feet would run down the wall from the planks above, seize a piece of liver that Dick had placed out for him and then scoot back up with his bloody prize.

Two days of warm rains (March 27th) and we knew that conditions were probably ideal for a wet night-time trip to the woodland pool way up in the swampy, back-forty cutover, a pool that serves for a very brief period once a year in the spring as a mating place for the spotted salamanders. With our flashlight beams reflecting the raindrops we sloshed our way along, constantly on the lookout for the large, bluish-black, yellow-spotted salamanders which were due to be moving toward their rendezvous. As we neared the big pool with its sphagnum-drenched logs, we began to see them — five in all. It is awesome to see one of them finally reach its destination and wiggle away in the black, cold pool, a furtive creature of land which returns by night to the water to reproduce, attaching its gelatinous mass of eggs to sticks or debris. When these hatch, the young gill-breathing salamander larvae live in the pool until transformation takes place; then they lose their gills and walk out onto land, sometime in August in this area.

For a few minutes we flicked off the flashlights and stood there allowing a world of absolute, total darkness to sink in while we wondered why we would walk so far and get so drenched just to see five salamanders crawling toward a pool. But in today's disrupted world, it was reassuring to know that the annual migration of the salamanders had not ceased.

March ended with the hibernating Compton tortoise shell and mourning cloak butterflies leaving their snug retreat in the hay bales while the deep yellow dandelion-like blossoms of the coltsfoot blanketed the freshly eroded roadside banks. Pure gold to a naturalist!

Very early April brought the large flocks of robins, meadow-larks, and blackbirds to the wet pasture; overhead were flights of whistling swans and circling vultures. Sixty-five turkey vultures returned this spring to our nearby roost, approximating last year's count.

Oh, those vultures! I was up on the bluff of the big woods stretched out quietly on the ground, partially hidden beneath the hemlocks and beeches hoping to watch the grouse drumming on his log in the creek valley below. I never did glimpse the grouse but I soon became aware of a different and unique kind of drumming; every few feet all about me were medium-sized ground spiders beating on dry brittle leaves with their palps. At times I could hear seven or eight arachnid tom-toms throbbing but I could not tell whether it was a courtship performance or a declaration of war — perhaps both. At any rate, I fell asleep in my warm, sheltered spot only to awake and find seven vultures perched in the trees above me, eyeing my motionless form. They departed as soon as they discovered I had discovered them — an unnerving experience for all of us!

Returning to the same lookout some days later I was rewarded once again, for this time a pair of wood duck came splashing down into the wide pool beneath me — the pool of the leaning hemlock and the five-spined stickleback fish. Unconscious of the grace and startling beauty they added to that woodland setting, their ruby eyes matching the clump of red trilliums growing beneath the old hemlock, they dipped and chased, and shook and preened. They were too much taken with one another to see me, so I was privileged to watch until they finally swam out of sight, floating, iridescent rainbows moving against clean, clear currents of water swirling over the sandstone.

They had paid no attention either to a woodchuck which cautiously moved down the bank to the bottomland to reach a spread of spring beauties. The woodchuck had passed up the yellow round-leaved violets and clumps of merry-bells blooming on the heaped earth near its den. What a delightful-sounding menu a woodchuck has to choose from! I could have remained there for hours more and, as always, it seemed incredible to me that more than four million people were within an hour's drive of Sawdust. Just before I stirred my stiffened legs into action, a winter wren and a ruby-crowned kinglet sang a spring-lovely duet. I was happy, too.

And May began. Baby woodcocks were already running behind their parent, while the scarlet tanagers, rosebreasted grosbeaks, Baltimore orioles, and wood thrushes were just claiming their nesting territories and mates. Here no courts decide marital altercations, but I watched a female oriole fighting her way out of a triangle by driving the intruding female down on top of a wide log and pounding her skull and body with such vicious jabs that even I cried out. About twenty minutes later the injured bird groggily departed.

Maroon-colored blossoms livened the pawpaw thickets and with them came the first zebra swallowtail butterfly. This magnificent species, more highly prized perhaps than any other native butterfly of this region, is an enticing challenge to photographers. A swift, erratic flyer, practically never coming to rest on a blossom, it is a difficult subject to photograph. I proceeded to solve this problem last year by going over to the pawpaw grove on Tupelo Hill and searching until I collected nine of their eggs, all found on the undersides of the pawpaw leaves. The first diminutive bristly caterpillar crawled out of its eggshell (which it ate) on June 15th, rested a bit, and then proceeded to eat the leaf of a pawpaw. Continuing to consume the fresh leaves that I provided daily, it eventually hung from a leaf by its unusual "skyhook" (the cremaster) as a newly transformed green chrysalid (pupa) on July 4th. Three of the nine chrysalids that formed were tan rather than green. I returned five of the chrysalids to the pawpaw grove and kept four outside at home. For months as I eyed the small, hanging, mummy-like pupae, I wondered if I would be fortunate enough to be there the moment one of them suddenly chose to split the chrysalid case and emerge as a butterfly. I was, for as they darkened I brought them inside, and on May 3rd the first moist, wrinkled, black-and-white striped butterfly righted itself with its spidery legs and proceeded to pump its life fluid into its folded wings. And what is more, Dick was not off discing or plowing with the tractor, but right there with his camera. A few hours later I had the joy of taking an adult zebra swallowtail back to the pawpaw patch and watching three hundred and three days of pupal patience fly free. The remaining three butterflies emerged the next day.

Another period of waiting ended with May 27th, for last winter, as blizzards raged outside, I was curled up by the fireplace reading Dr. Craig's book, *The Song of the Wood Pewee*. In it he completely and enthusiastically described a pre-dawn song of the wood pewee. Knowing only the clear, plaintive daytime pee-a-wee and the few twilight phrases, I realized I was curled up by woodland's finest musical treats by not getting into the woods early enough; by early enough, I mean three-thirty. So I went, and as I walked down that black, silent trail I was sorry that I hadn't been able to talk anyone in the family into going with me, for it was just plain scary at that hour. But once I heard the pewee's first little note I was all right. He sang continuously until daylight first seeped through the woods and the musical waves of other bird songs drowned him out. However, for a while he had the whole still valley to himself, filling it with such sweet exquisitely phrased music; surely to the least conspicuous and dullest-colored male bird in the valley has been given the finest voice. I finally remembered my thermos of hot coffee and silently drank a toast to all of them who sang with the promise of sunshine in their hearts, and to Dr. Craig for writing his book.

By then the morning was warming, too, rousing a bumblebee from its night-time grasp on a timothy stalk while a ruby-throated hummingbird took an early morning bath on top of the glistening dew-laden sumac leaves. I slowly returned home to begin my day's work.

Snapping turtle

LETTER THREE: *Summer 1970*

EACH YEAR IT HAPPENS in early June as I am preparing the evening meal. A dark velvety form beats past the kitchen window, and then another one, and soon a third, until — absurdly — I have come to associate promethea moths with peeling potatoes. But I immediately know that a female promethea must have crawled from a slim cocoon which had dangled all winter from a sassafras branch just outside the window. After discharging a few drops of liquid, she would quietly wait there for a mate to find her. This astonishing liquid, while it has no odor to me, is so attractive to the male prometheas that their feathery, perceptive antennae will pick up the scent as it is blown in the wind for as far as a mile away. (What a veritable chemist she is and how perfume manufacturers could use the likes of her!) At any rate, this year as in others, dinner forgotten, we all gathered to view once again one of nature's most extraordinary phenomena.

The males came in from the woods rather high over the house and past the sassafras tree that contained the female. Then they slowed down and began to retrace their flight. Within minutes they had dropped down to within a few feet of the female, and then down to inches. For awhile we brushed prometheas from our faces until one joined with the female. We quickly attempted to capture the rest of the males so that we could band and then release them. It is the only time we ever see these large moths for they do not come to our lights at night, although twice a closely related species, the tulip-tree silk-moth *(C. angulifera)* has come to the porch light.

While thinking of lepidoptera, perhaps I should tell you now another incredible tale. This one concerns the strong, beautiful, orange and black monarch butterfly. Intensive studies have been and are being conducted on this species; as part of the research project, many folk all over Canada and the United States are voluntarily tagging these butterflies with small paper bands hoping to determine their migratory habits. Last year Milcey and I banded over nine hundred monarchs; neither of us ever failing to whisper softly "come back" as the released butterfly pushed against our fingers and with a surge of power sailed out high and fast. And one almost did make it back! After being caught and tagged at Sawdust last July 26th, he probably cruised southwest until winter found him someplace along the southern boundary of our country. He would have passed the months there until the days lengthened and some instinctive spirit moved him to return north. With worn wings, he was still able to span the blue skybridge all the way back to Canonsburg, Pennsylvania, where this spring he was recaptured and returned by mail to the Toronto University, one of the very few insects known to make such an amazing journey!

While June 9th ended with the promethea moths, the next day began with dew drops and wood thrushes. For me, it is unthinkable to remain in bed when the wood thrush's rolling notes chime in through the open window. He is witnessing the loveliest time of another day and I must, too; dawn may be shared by all beating hearts. If it cannot be seen, it can be smelled or it can be felt as the cool air is warmed by the golden-fingered sun, and always it can be heard. Sneaking out of the house, past the reproachful eyes of Lisa (I dare not take her with me during the nesting season) I headed for the trail behind the barn. There I was halted, for who can walk past nickering horses? As I grained them, I paused to thank the phoebes, which had plastered a nest on the beam above Bel-Ray Helene's stall, for the time they spent chasing the flies and gnats. We never need spray.

I continued on down a steep bank to the main creek, which I followed until I arrived at the spot where a smaller creek tumbled into it. This place we call Moonshine Gulch, for rumor has it that years and years ago there was a lively still operation going on there. It is remote and lovely, with large Goldie's fern and narrow-leaved spleenwort, patches of shining club moss *(L. lucidulum)*, jewelweed wood nettles, towering black cherry, yellow birch, and hemlock trees. While I noticed eight species of warblers singing, I did not hear the one I was listening for — a Kentucky warbler. (It had to be a coincidence that he chose that particular gulch on Sawdust to frequent.) For days he had been singing; however, I never sighted a female and with each passing day, the chances of finding a nest seemed more remote. It would have been such an interesting record for this part of Ohio!

From my chosen spot, though, there was much more to be seen. A tiny shrew nervously ran in and out of the tangled, matted roots overhanging the bank of the creek. I was nervous, too, for I knew that about fifty feet away there was a Louisiana waterthrush nest with five newly-hatched babies that would be eaten if the shrew kept on going. However, it left the bank and darted away toward a massive, rotting log.

I sat there thinking about shrews and moles, with their elongated snouts and their mode of living. Since they are almost always in tunnels of dirt and dust and leaf mold, I wondered if they frequently sneezed. Biologists might very appropriately study the filter system their air passages and lungs must have. Another animal appeared, this time a medium-sized raccoon; after lapping a drink of water, it hunched its way over to and up a large tree. But from the spread of that tree it carefully crossed over branch by branch to a second tree where it disappeared into a large cavity. I wondered if perhaps there were young coon there and the parent was making certain it left no scented trail leading to the den tree for anxious dogs and hunters to follow, for too frequently no raccoon season is observed here by the local Daniel Boones. The birds all raised a chipping fuss as the coon moved about, for they know a natural enemy, but shortly they resumed singing. As I almost absentmindedly slapped at the mosquitoes, I attempted to decide which bird song was the most enchanting; when the veery whirled down the scale, he received my vote.

On my way home, I happened on a large snapping turtle which was languidly moving along the trail. They always appear mean and miserable to me, but this one especially so, for squads of mosquitoes swarmed about his neck and legs, competing with the leeches for his blood. Neither of us paused. The day before, though, Dick and I had spent about three hours watching two huge snapping turtles grappling together in our pond. It was probably the grimmest, most ferocious, yet silent battle either of us had ever seen on Sawdust. Over and over they writhed, first one on top of the water and then the other, never loosening a hold on one another, but using their claws and jaws until the water was streaming blood and frothy bubbles from gaping neck wounds. As those two reptiles heaved their way up and down the pond with small waves surging against the cattails, I looked around and realized how unconcerned most of the pond's inhabitants were. The downy woodpecker went right on feeding its noisy young in the old willow stub, a water snake never slid from its branch low over the water, and the little whitefaced dragonfly *(L. intacta)* returned over and over again to its resting spot on a certain leaf. Strange in a way, for the snake, the turtle, the bird, and the dragonfly have inched their way together through countless millions of years, yet with no communication between them other than to devour one another if the chance arises. I have to believe that man, an amateur on this planet's stage, will learn to do better.

Although the policy at Sawdust is not to take sides in nature, it is difficult for me to adhere to this rule when it concerns the birds against the black rat snakes. When, for example, I see a tiny bird like a house wren valiantly defending its nest against a six-foot serpent, I usually call for Dick to come and remove the snake. One wren nest we watched had six eggs in it. A black snake crawled in and took four of the eggs before Dick could remove it to a cage. Immediately following that, the wrens again began to scold. Investigating, Dick discovered a second large black rat snake in the box, and the two remaining eggs gone. This snake was put in jail, too. Shortly after, the wrens were still fussing and this time two more huge snakes were in the next box, one of them striking out at the wrens as they flew up to the box, while another snake was on the ground beneath the box. So we ended up with five black rat snakes, which we donated to the Black Hawk Indian Dancers. Hardly a dent in the rat snake population, however, for another creep of snakes (six this time) climbed up two adjoining apple trees and within an hour emptied out a robin, cedar waxwing, and chipping sparrow nest, while I stood by watching helplessly. Needless to say, though, we have no rats around the farmyard, for the black rat snake is well named.

Bluebird

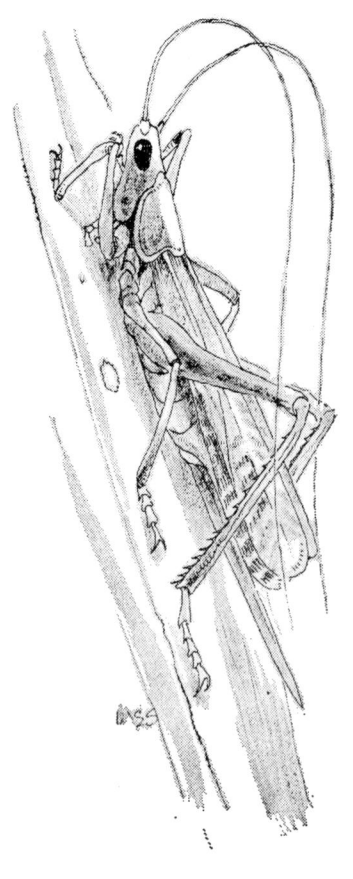

Coneheaded grasshopper

Letter Four: *Fall 1970*

To LIVE ON A FARM is truly to appreciate the autumn of each year. Its beauty and bounty linger in the aroma of apples stored in the cold cellar on the edge of the wooded ravine, in the pile of golden ears heaped in the corn crib, in the treasure of wild grape jelly beneath the paraffin caps, and in the mind which never forgets the glory of the autumn leaves. A sense of urgency is shared with the chipmunks as they carry cheekfuls of winter food into their earthen granaries, or with the honey bees as they turn the goldenrod and aster nectar into amber honey.

There is a restlessness about that is almost unnerving to me as I pass through the fields and woods, for everywhere the animal world is moving. Light tan shield bugs are climbing down the trunks of trees; tiny lonesome-sounding, piping spring peepers are searching for winter shelter in the woodlot's damp earth; wooly-bear caterpillars travel across the driveway and the paths on each warm sunny day, moving so rapidly I wonder just how great a distance one journeys before it curls up for the winter beneath a rock or slab of wood; southward waves of cabbage butterflies dance low over the fields; high in the sky are the mountain butterflies going southwest and above them are circling buteos, or suddenly the sky is filled with the dark swooping forms of nighthawks. Even the ruffed grouse act strangely, as some leave the woods and fly crazily about; this fall, as has happened three other autumns, a grouse dashed itself against a barn window. And those red squirrels! They never walk any place, they leap or jump like so many youngsters with springs on their tiny feet. The most constant movement of all, though, is the gentle drifting down of the colored leaves — one at a time, species by species, until the landscape is bare with the exception of the aspens and the willows, and finally they too lose their golden crowns.

The mysterious unseen forces that appear to control so much of the natural world especially add to the intrigue of autumn. Each year on a certain day, all over the farm and all over neighborhood farms, almost all of the paper wasps desert their inverted nests and proceed to hunt their old winter homes. Though it is hot and sunny, with no hint of winter, they will begin to climb into haylofts, attics, and sheds.

While the season's work of the wasps is obviously ended, it is just beginning for the linden moth *(Erannis tiliaris)*. On cold, late autumn nights, these wingless black-and-white female moths slowly move up the tree trunks to await the arrival of the winged males. With black needle-like ovipositors, the females thrust their clumps of yellowish orange eggs into the bark crevices. These eggs will hatch the following May and tiny caterpillars, commonly called inch-worms, will dangle on whitish, silken threads from the leaves and branches, choice food for migrating warblers and vireos. They are useful too for the Acadian flycatchers, who use the sticky threads to adorn and hold together their flimsy-looking, yet durable, nests. The caterpillar webs trail from a nest, trapping beech buds and old leaves on the sticky substance until the nest looks ancient and deserted.

It is somewhat ironic that the adult moths emerge so late in the season that they escape the migrating birds only to have their progeny gobbled up in the spring. The adults are not wholly safe, however, for I have seen chickadees and titmice diving after the male moths; green immature hemiptera piercing and sucking the helpless female moths; and I am confident the curved, sharp bill of the brown creeper must pick out some of the eggs as the creeper spirals its way up a tree trunk. (I often wonder how many times a day the brown creeper starts from the bottom, in its search for life anew.)

Autumn sounds hardly compare with those of spring and early summer but, to the attentive ear, they are an important part of fall nights and days. The coneheaded grasshopper *(Neoconocephalus ensiger)* begins to sing in the fields just as the bobolinks are departing. As in the other long-horned grasshoppers, the sound is produced by rubbing the two forewings together. The conehead is a common insect in fields and may often be heard over the roar of the motor while one is driving down the highway; sometimes people think that their car motor is making an abnormal sound that comes and goes as they pass from one singing grasshopper to another.

The loudest voice of all the orthoptera is that of the true katydid *(Pterophylla camellifolia)* which is heard singing from the lofty tree tops. It lives in the forest canopy and is ordinarily quite difficult to see or capture. It is often mistaken for its relatives, the bush katydids. Since the true katydid cannot fly, its movements are somewhat limited and where isolated woodlands are sprayed, it is often completely extirpated.

The incessant songs of the tree crickets provide the background for the orthopteran chorus which consists of approximately two dozen species here. The only colony of the temperature cricket *(Oecanthus niveus)* we have found on Sawdust is just outside our bedroom window in the sprawling bushes of the purple-flowering raspberry. We wait each fall for the first one to start singing. Like all other tree crickets, it raises its translucent wing covers until they are perpendicular and by rubbing them together it produces the sound and a very pretty sight, too, if we can manage to shine a flashlight on it without frightening it. Since insects are cold-blooded, their activity depends on the temperature, and the higher the temperature, the more active the insects are. Because of this, the air temperature may be obtained by counting the number of chirps per minute of this species, then subtracting forty, dividing that by four, and then adding fifty. Do not ask me who devised such a formula but it is surprisingly accurate.

Every day's walk becomes a search for a colored memory. I return each fall to certain places simply to enjoy once again the beauty; a witchhazel bush that uncurls its tousled, yellow autumn blossoms against the rich green branches of a hemlock; a clump of bright red tupelo trees shining in the early morning sunrise; parchment-like black cherry leaves, eighty feet high, massed against a full moonlit sky; or the most flamboyant color extravaganza of all, an old stand of sumac.

I sought out the sumac today. Its scarlet pennants were just as vivid as last year, with masses of yellow wild grape leaves in their midst and tall clumps of New England aster splashing purple below. And then I heard a catbird sing — so faint, so perfect, and so beautiful with all the spring fervor and length but just a symphonic shadow — a whisper song. Another memory whispered then to me across the decades, and I was thirteen years old. I could see me trying to find another catbird singing just that way and remember my utter disbelief when I realized the catbird was on a branch just above my head, for it was the first time I had ever witnessed a whisper song. The melodies in nature do not change, I thought, but people do. Then it returned—a chilling conversation of a few weeks ago — and it, too, concerned thirteen-year-olds. A friend was telling me that her sister had assigned an "in-class" theme to her seventh grade class; they were to write on what they thought the year 2000 would be like. Upon correcting the papers, she found that more than eighty percent of the children had written that there would be nobody here in the year 2000! What have we done to the optimism of our children?

I tried putting the thought out of my mind as I walked home for it took the joy out of the loveliness I had been seeking. I thought of tonight's menu — eggplant stuffed with shrimp and rice; I examined strange, apricot-colored, small, tumor-like fungi, with bright, bittersweet, colored juice oozing out and running down, hardening like candle drippings; I crushed the emerald leaf of a young sweet cicely plant and it smelled of anise and that made me think of Christmas; there is always new hope at Christmas time. The wild movement of a leaf caught in a cobweb line made an intriguing flourish as the wind danced with it; it became a marionette cavorting, with nature pulling the invisible strings. Nature will forever pull the strings of mankind and someday if we are too contemptuous of this she will pull the noose — fast and sure. No, I could not forget, but I believe man is awakening to this and will improve his ways. He must!

Least shrew

Red-shouldered hawk

👁 👁 LETTER FIVE: *Spring 1971*

ONE DAY IN EARLY APRIL: Winter's many silent days no longer grip Sawdust. From the valley the creek may be heard forcing its way through tangled sticks, fallen logs, over the sedge beds and boulders. A phoebe calls from behind the barn and a song sparrow, head tipped back, sings again and again from the top of the apple tree opposite the house. On one of the fence posts separating the pasture from the hay field perches a caroling meadowlark; robins — so fat, so beautiful, so welcome — battle vociferously for territories, while a pair of bluebirds fly about one of the bird houses in the old vineyard.

The thread of life is unwinding once again on the farm as so many lovely melodies are being sung, as some of the buds are spreading into delicate green fans, and as the winter-hard ground is turning into soft mud. And in my rubber boots I find myself going out of my way to walk through the very muddiest spots I can find. Later on, I appreciate the drier soil as I fine it through my fingers and help Dick plant the garden, but right now the strong pull of the oozy, slippery mud against my boots means the things that fascinate me so will be appearing once more.

So many new study projects are to be started, so many old ones to be continued, and so many splendid things to be seen. I presume it is all in one's point of view, but to me absolute perfection is to be found only in the natural world and it is for the rare glimpse of this that I continue to walk and probe the place we call Sawdust. Perfection, not just in beauteous forms, but in the life processes. To study the delicate, seemingly bizarre and astounding arrangements attained by animals and plants so that they may hold their own place here, means spending my days in a state of incredible, wondrous bewilderment. The very tiny forms intrigue me the most, perhaps, for they appear to live against such insurmountable odds.

Now that our creek is ice-free, I turn toward it to search for some of the curious forms found there. In many places the water is too high for wading, but already water striders are scooting across these wide, deep pools, the oval shadows of their six feet moving beneath them. The reflections are actually shadows of the dimpling of the water by the insects' feet. This large slender insect with very long middle and hind legs lives only on the surface of the water; if submerged, other than momentarily, it will drown. Apparently it is kept afloat and dry by a fine coating of hairs and by the air collected in those hairs. Water striders must hibernate along the creek but I have never been able to find them during the winter.

In the shallower stretches of the creek, where a riffle tumbles fast over some rocks, I wade out to check for the presence of small (five millimeters long) caddisfly cases. They are there, slight cornucopias of sand crystals, with the narrow ends all pointing downstream and the single caddisfly larva within each case holding firmly to the rock with its protruding feet. I count fifty-nine of these little stone houses on one rock slab and I wonder at the uniformity of the size and color and structure of each case. I do not know how many crystals of quartz are used to make up each case, but I do know that they are solidly constructed and that the secretion used by the larvae to cement the tiny rock particles together must be a fine waterproof substance. If I were a chemist I am certain I would be analyzing this secretion. Each species of caddisfly has its own particular type of case. One species will use bits of debris, another green blades of grass or round pebbles, but each caddisfly spends its larval and pupal stages in the water before emerging from its pupal case as an adult to fly airborne.

In the same spot, also needing swirling, churning, clean water, there is another kind of insect larva clinging to a rock, the larvae of buffalo gnats. How different they are from the caddisfly larvae: no snug home around their naked, dingy, yellowish-white, almost cylindrical bodies (six to seven millimeters long), all facing with heads downstream while they hang on to the rock with their swollen tails.

There are one hundred and fifty-two of them arranged in neat rows across the face of one rock, a helpness company of tiny soldiers that have very little protection against the onslaught of a hungry rainbow or fantail darter, should one swim up the riffle. I discover what the larvae might do against such a predator as I dislodge a few of them. Those remaining drop from the rock, seeming to spin a thread out as they leave. Later on they loop back on this slim life line to the rock. These larvae, I know, have many unique adaptations for in previous years I have taken some home to study and to keep in a heavily aerated aquarium until the wide-eyed hump-backed dark adult gnats emerge.

They are able to maintain their precarious hold onto the rock because each larva has a disc with many, many tiny hooks on the end of its tail and, in addition, places a sticky secretion on the rock. They hang there, in the swift current, waiting for plankton and organic matter to be carried by which they gather into their mouths by means of two brushlike fans with thirty to sixty cured rays. After several moults, the larvae, looking like weavers as they move their heads back and forth, spin their pupal cases. When finished, they are covered by a white silken net pouch, and as the pupal stage is reached two respiratory filaments, reminding me of a set of antlers, protrude from the anterior end of the cocoon. All of this I have seen, but what happens next — the most crucial and ingenious part of the cycle — I have missed. Because the adult gnat will drown in water, some way had to be evolved to get it out of the submerged pupa and up to the air. This is accomplished by a bubble of air which is formed around the fly within the pupa and which then escapes to the surface of the water and pops, ejecting the gnat out into the air. Perhaps this year I will be lucky enough to see the actual moment when the little bubble of air, encasing the gnat, rises from a pupa. And now I will tell you, buffalo gnats are also called black flies — those demoniacal, blood-thirsty flies that make the northern woods a miserable place to be for part of the summer. Placing some rocks with some of the larvae in a pail of water, I am ready to go home, but standing there with the clear, cold water spraying against my boots I hear a red-shouldered hawk above the valley. The buteo, with wings half-bent, dives straight down, its screaming cry and feathered force cleaving the bright blue spring sky. He helps to warm my toes as I leave the frigid water, and so do a flock of juncos gently trilling as they move about in a tangle of grapevines.

 Once home, the gnat larvae are placed in an aquarium where they soon loop their way from the rock to the aerator itself. Dinner is prepared and eaten, the dishes stacked, and I leave the house once more.

 This time I wish that everyone I know and those I do not know could join me for one of the most faultless, enchanting nocturnal performances on Sawdust. To attend, I need only walk a short distance up the driveway any nice spring evening and sit down beside an old chestnut fence post in the ancient vineyard, now overgrown with young red maples, quaking aspens, meadowsweet, and weeds. As the day merges into night but while there is still enough afterglow to see—the awaited performer, a woodcock, flies in and lands less than fifty feet from me. This inland sandpiper, with his large shoe-button eyes, short legs, virtually no neck, and very long bill, is in no hurry for the curtain to rise. He carefully preens each wing with his lengthy bill and then all the rest of his body, interrupting the job occasionally with a nasal "beep" which sounds so much like the cry of a nighthawk. Suddenly his mood seems to change, and he begins calling "beep beep beep beep" over and over again, and before each loud "beep" he delivers a softer sound through his closed bill.

Usually I am too far away to hear that muted note. I count his calls, as I would unconsciously count a chiming clock — one hundred and two. Then, abruptly, he pushes away from the ground and flies across the vineyard. I lose sight of him until he mounts higher in the air and is silhouetted against the sky. With rapid wing beats he begins to circle, passing over a corner of the pasture, the driveway, a little of the orchard, and then he is passing over me again. On he sweeps in a series of spirals ascending higher with each circle. I cannot always see him but I am able to trace his movements by his constant twittering. When he reaches a height of about one hundred and fifty feet the moment comes that is so magical. The twittering ceases, there is a pause until he begins to pour forth his true song — a potpourri of sweet warbled chirps — unlike any other bird music I know. He repeats his song several times as he descends in a wild, erratic, zigzag fashion, ending as he glides into the far edge of the vineyard. From that hidden part of his singing territory he resumes his calling. Twelve more "beeps" and he ascends once more to repeat his aerial courtship. For the next thirty minutes his ethereal flights continue, and when they finally stop I realize that night has fallen, and the earth-sky fantasia is ended for this evening.

Wood frog

Male bobolink

🐂 🐂 LETTER SIX: *Summer 1971*

PERSONAL MEMORIES, TREASURED THOUGHTS of happy times and moments impossible to repeat, so often become blurred and worn.

How different for the natural world, where each year nature, if permitted, relives her memories with styles and ways unchanged. This reaffirmation of the continuity of life attracts students of nature; the old and familiar is revered, not repudiated, while the unknown is vigorously pursued.

I know that the years will not dim the summer night lights or the fireflies as they shift above the pond, so many flickering little stars reflected in the black water, nor will the bullfrogs, those after-dinner speechmakers, be stilled. The flaming pillars of cardinal flower along a creek bed will forever brighten a July day just as the blue wheels of chicory blossoms bear the sky down to a summer morning roadside. Butterflies will casually move about in fields and shady copses while feathered minstrels entertain with song. Clouds won't hide the sun from the fields of goldenhearted daisies; indeed, I am happy that a field of daisies is ever a cause for rejoicing, not just a dream of yesterday.

For some species a break in this continuity has occurred as a result of man's interference. One bird that has become just a memory here on Sawdust is the marsh hawk. When we first moved here, a pair nested on the ground a few hundred feet from the house in a wet, weedy field. I wish I could fully describe the beauty of their aerial courtship flights or the grace of their wing movements as they circled the field in search of food, tipping their wings like large gulls. Just adjacent to the field, our silver-spangled hamburg bantam chicks were running free, and though we rather expected the marsh hawks occasionally to take one of these tiny chicks, they never did. Once I watched the female hawk drop down in the midst of the scattering bantams, but she arose dangling instead a garter snake. Now, it has been several years since I have seen a marsh hawk flying across any field in our township.

But, we still have the upland plovers! The trustees of our Trumbull Township (a township with a meager population, two hundred *fewer* people than the census of 1870 recorded) could properly boast that this township is the summer home for a score of upland plovers — birds that journey almost eight thousand miles from another hemisphere to nest in our fields.

I visit these fields frequently for they are one of the nicest places to hail the sunbeams of a newly fledged June day. Rolling gently in waves, the long grasses of the hayfield protect a teeming variety of life. An upland plover carefully folds its wings as it settles on the rounded top of a nearby rural telephone pole. Moments before, it had been expressing its alarm with loud, rapid ip-ip ip's as it circled over me. I am content to remain on the edge of the field for I just came to listen and to watch. And to smell, for the aroma of a hayfield in the sun is very special. Soon the morning air is filled with the rich, mellow, yet somewhat mournful song of the plover. I have yet to read a perfect description of its song — it must be heard to appreciate the haunting quality, but once you have listened to it you will never forget it.

While the upland plover is the meadow's greatest pied-piper, other birds, rising and falling with their songs, help hold the tempo of the meadow life. A horned lark, leaving the ground, mounts high in the sky and delicately twists out his tinkling notes almost unnoticed in this world of sound. Then, rapidly dropping to the ground after about two minutes of high circling singing, the small troubadour resumes his mousy way of running amongst the grassy and weedy terrain. Several bobolinks claim this meadow, too. Clinging to the weed tops or bursting high above the field with their rollicking, bubbling songs, these black and white birds seem to have the enthusiasm of an old-time organ grinder. But no agile monkey comes over with its tin cup to collect those coins. So the only way I can repay the bobolinks is to try to keep the moving machine out of the field until their young are able to fly. I realize that the old man who occasionally came by many years ago with his music and monkey has vanished forever, but please, not the bobolinks!

And the sparrows are here, too; they will abide this field for two or three months after the plovers and bobolinks have left for the pampas of Argentina. The field sparrow, with its sweet peals of song, guarantees constant music on even the hottest days. It appears to be a light sleeper for so often its silvery notes part the nighttime quiet. One little field sparrow will never be forgotten by four of us at Sawdust for he played a part in one of the most stunning and unplanned spectaculars we have ever witnessed here.

It was about eleven o'clock at night and we were all outside, a small cluster of people watching the sky. All of us had seen northern lights flickering before, but none of us had ever seen such a display as that night. It was as though we were in an immense tent with the entire canopy a shooting, trembling, and rippling ceiling of light waves. In the midst of this magnificent, almost supernatural celestial display, a lone field sparrow awoke and as the erratic colored lights danced above, it sang and sang. Somehow we were locked together for life by this song, a fusion of earth, heaven, and loved ones. An "Amazing Grace"!

Another sparrow of this field that is often heard at night is the Henslow sparrow, the afterthought of the bird world. He sings now in the field but his song is a mere tick of time — a single penetrating sslick — never more, never less than that, hardly to be called a song. He sits on a weed just a few inches from the ground and, if jostled from his perch, barely flies above the grasses. Nature seems to have humbled him even more, for he has a big flat head and stubby tail, and nothing but olive or brownish feathers. Three more species of sparrows may be counted as the two-syllable, weak, buzzing trill of the grasshopper sparrow is heard and the spirited chants of the song and vesper sparrows sound from the field's edge.

As I meadow-watched, the persistent call of a least flycatcher carried across from the wooded edge of the grassy acreage. Finally I crossed over to the stand of aspen, grapevines, bird cherry, and brambles to see if by any chance there actually was a nesting pair of the flycatchers there, for I had never found a nest pair of that species on Sawdust. Eventually I did locate their nest, a compact structure in the crotch of a sugar maple sapling, too high to see what it contained. Excited, I hurried home to tell Dick of my discovery.

While June's bucolic fields beckon on a sunshiny day, we await cloudy, sultry summer evenings to go sugaring for moths in the woodland valley. An attempt is made to keep a mixture of brown sugar and stale beer on hand so that when the weather conditions seem right, we are prepared with a sweetened brew. This ancient technique, used by professional and amateur entomologists, guarantees a fascinating night in the woods. We have long used it, not just to collect species of insects, but to teach Rick and Milsey as small children to love the nocturnal woods. As a result, we have a fine collection of the genus *Catocala* (underwing moths) and the children, now grown, think nothing of curling up in a sleeping bag alone on a Montana mountainside or a plain in Wyoming.

We missed the enthusiasm of the kids the other night as we took our sweetened mixture and a brush and proceeded to walk the loop trail just before dusk. Every so often Dick would smear the grown, fermented mixture on the side of a big tree or old stump, until the small pail was empty. Later on after dark, carrying a camera, we retraced our route to see what insects had found the sticky, odoriferous trickles. As many seasons as we have done this, I still am full of anticipation as we cautiously approach a painted tree and direct the flashlight beam to the spot, hoping to see some large moths there. The first few stops showed only excited ants and small moths but as we came to the fifth smeared tree a large underwing moth (three inches) landed on the side of the tree. Dick managed to photograph it before it closed its fore wings, which hide its brilliant scarlet and black hind wings. It was a species known as the Once-married Underwing (*Catocala unijuga*) which we had previously collected so we made no attempt to capture it. Before the evening was ended we had photographed two more species, the Sleepy Underwing (*C. concumbens*) with pink and black hind wings, and the Penitent Underwing (*C. piatrix*) with deep yellow and black hind wings. There are many more species of underwing moths and the early scientists naming them must have had a marvelous sense of humor for they chose names such as The Sweetheart, The Oldwife, The Tearful, The Dejected, The Widowed, The Darling, The Inconsolable, The Gloomy, The Pure, The Bride, The Little Wife, The Youthful, The Serene, The Wayward, The Polygamist. In addition to photographing the moths, we collected an amazing beetle, of the tribe Cychrini. It was thirty-four millimeters long, with extremely large elytra and a very slender head and pronotum. This species is one of a small group of snail-eating beetles which, because of their very long, thin heads, are able to extract the soft parts of the snail from their coiled shells. (The species we found, using Blatchey's classification, was *Cychrus viduus*.)

As we walked home a whippoorwill was calling and then we heard the unusual repetitious notes of a barred owl. Not the usual hoots or wild cry, but rather a wistful, repeated whistle that began low and ended up on a higher pitch. To imitate it, one has to whistle backwards, that is — you draw in your breath. For five years we occasionally heard these notes in the woods but never knew what animal or bird was making them. Then one spring while watching a barred owl on her nest of eggs, I heard her begin calling and the mystery was solved.

That nest of barred owls, incidentally, met its end in a peculiar fashion. It was in an exposed cavity and the incubating bird half stood and leaned against the two white eggs. One day as Dick was watching the nest through a telescope across the ravine, the parent bird left and moments later a fox squirrel quietly moved in, taking first one egg and then the second. The battle for survival goes on, just another link in nature's continuous chain of life.

Jewel weed (Touch-me-not)

LETTER SEVEN: *Fall 1971*

I AM WRITING THIS AS I SIT on an old beech tree log which fell here in 1956. Fairly solid, with none of its gray bark left on, it is an ideal bench for me, since I am able to look down on the two creeks and a wide portion of the flood plain. From here I have watched a mother raccoon and her young ones agilely pulling down ripe blackberries to feast on, and a crow taking a young robin from its nest and calmly devouring part of it there on the ground in spite of the frenzied shrieks and accurate dive bombings of the parent robins. Hardly daring to move, I saw from here for the first time in my life a ruffed grouse drumming. First amazed at how high he lifted his wings and how fast he raised and lowered them, shock replaced amazement when a fox suddenly appeared and with a catlike pounce went after the grouse. The fox missed and then, seemingly bewildered by its failure, ran back and forth on the log, twitching its bushy tail. Another day a fox squirrel steadily swimming downstream intrigued me: it had found a fine way to cool itself or possibly to help rid itself of fleas. Then there was a woodchuck which reached up and pulled over stalk after stalk of wood-nettle, apparently impervious to the stinging hairs as he slid the stalks and leaves into his mouth. When I so much as brush my wrist or hand against that plant, I search immediately for a touch-me-not (jewel weed) plant so I can squeeze some of its juice on my skin to halt the itching and burning caused by the nettle. It is unfortunate that the nettle plant has this protective device for, as a food, it is very high in protein, higher than alfalfa.

Just this last week from this vantage point I observed a crow for about fifteen minutes as it performed a special kind of grooming, that of "anting," or rubbing its feathers with crushed ants. At first I thought the crow was entangled in a vine as it flopped and struggled there on the ground, but as I continued to stare, I realized what it was doing. Standing with its legs well apart amidst the ant colony, the bird extended and bent its wings and pushed its head forward and down. I could not tell from where I was watching whether the crow was picking the ants up and rubbing them on its feathers beneath its wings and on its breast, or whether the disturbed ants running up and over the crow discharging their poison were then picked out and crushed as the bird preened. At any rate, it was a most interesting procedure and after the crow flew, I hastened down to see what was there. The crow had used what seemed to me to be a small colony of medium-sized yellowish ants, and a very pungent odor remained at the spot along with many mashed ants. One may speculate whether the chemical from the ant is used by the crow as a feather preservative or insect repellent, or perhaps, who knows, there may be no purpose behind the ritual — some birds might just like to sniff the formic acid which is found in the bodies of ants.

A hooded warbler just broke the vast silence here with a short lightsome song: how late he has lingered, for usually they are well on their way to Central America by now. Certainly he will travel farther from Sawdust this year than I expect to do. We had fewer hooded warblers nesting here this past summer than usual but it was interesting that for the third season I found one of their nests cradled in the forked stem of a black cohosh plant. Well, anyway, I hope his tiny wings will carry him to his winter home and then back to grace our ravines once more.

In a dim, damp spot below, the sprawling plants of spotted cowbane or water-hemlock, with their seeded heads, are turning yellow. These plants should be eradicated for they are deadly poisonous. Scores of children and adults have died in this country from eating its tuberous roots or its leaves and this was the plant that was used by the Indians when they chose to commit suicide. A close relative of the water-hemlock known as poison hemlock has been introduced into this country from Europe and is now commonly found in waste areas all over the United States and Canada. The juice of this plant was supposed to have been used by the early Greeks to kill criminals, just as the gas chamber or the electric chair is used now. (Socrates was made to swallow this extract.) Both of these plants are in the parsley family and they closely resemble a wild carrot or Queen Anne's lace when it is in bloom. When the children were very young and yet had the freedom to roam Sawdust, I used to worry that they would disobey the one rule we made so much of — *never* eat anything in the woods or fields! We didn't fret about falls, stings, poison ivy, snakes, or getting lost, but the many poisonous berries, mushrooms, and other plants were an important cause for concern. And how attractive the berries are right now: the red berries of the Solomon's-plume, the orange ones hanging on the yellow mandarin, the deep blue of the blue cohosh fruit, and the tight cluster of scarlet berries on the Jack-in-the-pulpit and ginseng. At this time of the year I always bring in stems of the purple nightshade vine, which will have lovely violet flowers as well as oval berries on it, and, before your very eyes, the berries will turn from green to yellow to orange to crimson; this would be ideal if someone were interested in making a delayed time-study movie.

About twenty feet from where I am resting, there is a precious stand of starflower, precious because it is the only place that I know of where they are growing on Sawdust and because its pointed petals form such an exquisite white star late in the spring. Perhaps I will find it some place else on our five hundred acres, just as I chanced upon a clump of ebony spleenwort fern the other day. Many years ago I had found one small plant of this fern on the farm but it eventually disappeared. I believe I can say that I have pretty well combed our land throughout the years, with the exception of about thirty acres. This one wild, jungly place I have carefully refrained from entering, attempting somehow to save a little bit of the unknown for myself. Perhaps I shall not find anything new to Sawdust when I at last go looking there, but, in the meantime, I can contemplate an orchid or two.

No mosquitoes today, but the bees are shining targets as they cross the shafts of sunlight and enter a hole in the ancient hemlock above me. Their honeycomb is almost protruding from the hole. The cavity was used by a fox squirrel to raise her family before the bees filled it, and it was originally chiseled out by a pileated woodpecker. Here on the log there is a steady procession of black ants. I am a nuisance to them. Ants are so much longer-lived than bees: a worker bee lasts only about six weeks, whereas a worker ant may live as long as six or seven years. A queen bee may remain active for several years but a queen ant may reign for as long as fourteen years.

A noisy band of chickadees and tufted titmice scatter themselves among the branches of one of the giants of Sawdust — a sycamore tree growing along the creek below. Fortunately spared by the lumbermen so long ago, it just keeps spreading itself up and mostly out. Today it is silent but usually there is enough wind to jostle its dried leathery leaves into quite a conversation, and I love it for that if for no other reason. Hundreds of seed balls are dangling from the top of the tree, and it always surprises me that the birds do not pull these buttonballs apart to eat the tiny fuzzy nutlike seeds. Rather, these balls swing up there for almost a year before the slim stem breaks off and you find the buffy balls broken apart and drifting down the creek in April and May. Their seeds require a constant supply of moisture to germinate, so I suppose that is why sycamores are usually found along river banks or in wet woodlands. Young sycamores have the most picturesque bark, for large patches of the outer bark peel off exposing the colored inner bark. One of the lesser puzzles to be solved here on the homeplace concerns sycamore trees. Just a few years ago I was caught in our woods during a tornado, and as I sped for home amid the roar and crashing branches, I noticed some bright, bright yellow tree trunks in the distance. I couldn't believe what I was seeing for it looked as though someone had been on a psychedelic painting spree in our woods. As scared as I was, I had to detour in the deluge to see what it was. There were three young sycamore trees with as vivid mustard yellow bark as I had ever seen, not the soft yellow or green they usually are. I have since returned to check those trees during every possible type of weather conditions: fogs, thunderstorms, freezing rains, snow, yet never have they been colored the way they were that day. Now I am awaiting another tornado and I just hope I shall have the courage to return and look them over. The barometer had fallen that day to the lowest point Dick had ever seen it plunge and of course I am wondering if the sycamores are a sort of natural woodland warning when you do not have a barometer to study. However, it might also have been due just to peculiar light conditions during that storm. Have you ever been out in the woods just before a tornado hits? Your first thought as the wind hits the treetops is that a convoy of army planes is passing overhead.

Today as I sit here, with not much but my thoughts stirring, there is ample time just to allow the beauty of the golden world about me to crowd out the somber thoughts that always seem to haunt me in an autumn woodland. Death seems so imminent and spring so far away, yet the creatures about me do not seem to concern themselves with either. Only man rejects the idea of dying just as only man is capable of hate. I believe that one of the most important reasons for the preservation of natural areas is to save some places where hate is non-existent. As fierce and desperate as the battle for survival is in nature, it is not to be confused with hate. Besides, it is difficult to hate when you have just spent the morning with a fringed gentian or followed the scarlet trail of a Virginia creeper vine.

Great-horned owl

LETTER EIGHT: *Winter 1971*

IT SEEMS BUT SUCH A BRIEF TIME AGO that lingering myrtle warblers were eating the grayish poison ivy berries or fluttering around the porch and windows snapping up house flies that crawled out as the November day warmed. Now, as a bleak storm rages outside, the yearly battle begins for me once more. I have to tell myself for a few months that it is the most beautiful time of all on the farm, that I enjoy being cold, that I would yearn desperately for snow and sunlit icicles if I were birding in the Rio Grande Valley, and that it is a quiet and remote life with time to read and be warmed by the hickory logs burning away in the fireplace. But in my heart, as I listen to the musical chatter of the tree sparrows outside, I find myself already straining to hear instead their high, clear, spring songs, wishing for the reassuring touch of spring.

Sometimes I have sense enough, though, to cease either looking back or ahead, and to enjoy completely what winter brings. Redpolls, for example! This year large, chatty, colorful flocks of them invaded our place, tilting the seeded heads of health aster and lamb's quarters plants. But just when they had captured my heart, they were gone — like so many holiday children.

And only winter could have bestowed one of the most electrifying sights of this year. So furiously was it snowing that morning when I left the house, Blackie failed for once to whinny; he simply could not see me coming. After I finished feeding him, I leaned against the barn door, idly studying the snowflakes as they came to rest on my arm. Lost seconds of time, crystal snowy moments melting away; for just a bit, I felt as though I might be holding secrets of eternity on my wooly coat sleeve. My reverie was abruptly shattered, though, as I heard whistling swans — distressed, bewildered-sounding swans. I had to believe my ears, for suddenly directly before me the snowy air was filled with long-necked, immense birds beating their way through the blizzard: twenty-one white jets about to land on the black waters of our pond, a wet dark oasis for them in that all-white world. For some reason, at the last minute they did not land; perhaps they wisely realized that the pond was too small. Somehow they righted themselves, regrouped, and continued on their southeast journey. I'm not positive that I counted them correctly nor do I recall breathing as they passed, but I must have for I had enough wind to dash into the house to tell Dick what I had just seen. Never before had I been so near to swans in flight and I was totally unprepared for just how gigantic they were. Seeing a seven-foot wingspread is much more impressive than reading about it. It was a very late date for swans to be seen here, as long lines of them had passed high overhead weeks before. The fall migration of swans is our timetable for snow tires and storm windows.

After years of not hearing or seeing horned owls about the farm, they have re-established themselves here. Usually we just hear their low hoots, but one night this winter our neighbor (our half-a-mile-away neighbor) arrived with a great horned owl perched on his arm. Our astonishment matched Frank's grin, since he knew how Dick had wished he could band one of the owls. He explained that the previous night the owl had killed one of his call ducks and then dragged it across the snow and cached it beneath some branches near the edge of their pond. So Frank placed a live trap there and when the owl returned the next night to feast on the dead duck, it was caught. It was a magnificent bird. Throwing our heavy coats on, and finding equally sturdy gloves, we all trooped out to the barn where the bird-banding equipment was kept. Dick and Frank worked together to place the band on its leg, while Ruth and I debated which husband the owl would strike first with its formidable talons. For the first time Dick was able to use a number nine band, which is the largest band the United States Fish and Wildlife Service supplies (the same size used for swans, eagles, and condors). Since Dick weighs most of the birds he bands, they had to wrap it up to place it on the scales (minus the twine, it weighed three an a half pounds). Usually I feel sorry for the frightened-looking birds as they are momentarily held captive, but I felt no pity this time, just admiration, for never was there a prouder, more poised prisoner than that owl. Bound and flat on its back, it still looked you squarely in the eye with no sound, no surrender. As soon as they had finished, they released it outside and it became once again the hunter, the mate, the parent homeward bound.

As the men handled the owl, several flat, yellowish-winged parasitic flies crawled from its feathers onto their coats. These insects were speedily collected and placed in vials. I had to look them up inasmuch as they were new to me and I found them to be louse flies of the family Hippoboscidae and genus *Olfersia*, which spend their lives on the bodies of birds of prey. The life history of this blood-sucking fly was interesting because the larvae remain within the body of the female fly until pupation is ready to take place.

Yesterday, with sunlight spilling over the whitened still valley, I stood there and wondered why I loved it so. Far more spectacular views may be found elsewhere, but it is home and it is good land and it is there to be quietly cherished, if nothing else. Sunshiny winter days usually find me along the big creek, where I have spent so much time through the years attempting to piece together the life histories of an order of small insects known as stone-flies (Plectoptera). They are one of the few insects which emerge as adults during the winter months. They spend their immature lives in the creek, but starting in December and on through March the different species will crawl from the icy stream and shed their nymphal skins and gills, to become air-breathing adults. They are less than half an inch in length, dark, flat, and narrow, with wings (if female), long antennae, and with two abdominal projections (cerci) which are almost as long as the antennae. Perhaps if I said that often they remind me of animated hemlock needles as they run over the snow, you would have a clearer picture of them. Hundreds will leave the creek at about the same time and then all will begin to scramble away from the creek, over mounds of snowy brush, down into deep icy crevices and up the other side, until finally they come to the ravine bank. Still not tiring apparently, the march goes on — up the eighty-foot hillside and continuing into the level woodland. At times some pause to nibble on the algae and green mossy patches found on the old stumps and often the tufted titmice and chickadees gather to feast on them. Yesterday I chose to follow just one of those stone-flies and discovered it took her three and one-half hours to reach the top of the ravine. It was primarily females that had emerged and left the water. The males tend to remain near the creek, but I think the females return to the creek to mate at a later time. The mating process appears to be a fairly dangerous procedure for them both. The smaller male climbs on the back of the female and she then proceeds to take them both as close to the swirling water as she can without tumbling in. But couple after couple are swept away, and unless they are lucky enough to be thrown against debris of some kind, they will drown. However, many eggs must get deposited, for each year new adults may be found climbing out over the slippery rocks.

As I followed the one stone-fly yesterday afternoon, I had ample time to examine other things, too. Round, red basswood buds — they must be one of the brightest, gayest spots of color in the winter woods, while the long, narrow, green, purplish-tipped buds of the red-berried elder shrub enticed me with their green folded wings of springtime-to-be. Also found were tiny springtails (Collembola) clustered around large tree roots, looking more like specks of black soot than small insects. To appreciate fully these very minute snow insects, I have to get down on my hands and knees and play with them. Tiddlywinks is the name of the game. They have a most curious habit of springing up and out when you touch them gently, for beneath their abdomen there is a tiny folded projection which, if straightened out, flips them across the snow for as much as two inches. One other day down in the floodplain, I was sprawled on the ground following these little springtails around the base of a tree, attempting to see just how far they actually could jump. I do not know how long I was doing this but the next day as I was walking along the opposite ridge of the valley, I saw where a trespassing fox hunter apparently had been standing in the snow above me and I couldn't help but wonder if he had been watching me as he waited up there for a fox to come down the valley.

Last evening as I sat typing, I listened to the tape of Mystic Moods with its recorded thunder storms and sea waves — sounding out the message "There's a Good Earth Out Tonight." I suddenly wondered what I was doing inside; my notes could wait. Dressed as though I were about to take a dogsled up the Chilkoot Pass, I stepped out on the frigid squeaky snow and into a magic world. All the unused Christmas glitter must have been spread over the orchards, the fields, the yard, the fences — everywhere icy crystals sputtered in the moonlight. Cold, bright light retraced each tree below on the snow, tree-tangled gray shadows of moontime. Warmed by the incredible world I found myself in, I felt as though I could walk forever. Perhaps I could have, but within an hour it began to snow, which soon hazed the moon and veiled the stars. However, even that added to the unusual, for suddenly a meteorite shot down low in the distant northern horizon. For a brief moment I did not comprehend what I had just seen —

a blazing shooting star in a snowstorm was rather like viewing lightning when the sun was shining. As I walked along without seeing any electric lights, I couldn't help but think of how the lighted city of Cleveland had appeared Sunday night as we drove along Route 71. Vibrant, vital, dynamic, bright, and beautiful, it glowed in the winter darkness. I should have liked to wander there, perhaps, but I am a stranger there now and afraid. The silent smog was ominous and during the journey home I repeatedly wondered if some morning perhaps nobody in the city would awaken.

Returning home on the trail that led past the cabin, I was almost tempted to go in and start up the old Home Comfort wood stove. And as I stood there in the cabin clearing I could see again the firelight and loved ones gathered around, taste the steaks with mushrooms flambeau, and hear the guitar music blending with evening choruses of katydids or wood thrushes as the children sang one of their favorite ballads, "The Circle Game." I left humming it, too: "and the seasons, they go 'round and 'round and the painted ponies go up and down."

American toad

LETTER NINE: *Spring 1972*

EACH DAY AS THE SUN MOUNTS a little higher in the sky, the roosters crow just a little earlier, and sugar snows give way to genial rains, there is not a foot of earth on this farm that does not include some living thing responding to the urge to thrust itself back into the warm spring of life. Everywhere winter-slowed hearts are gently speeded up, eyelids are rolled back, wings and antennae meticulously cleaned, muscles flexed, legs stretched, mouth parts tested, pupal skins split, curled bodies straightened, or fur pelts freshened as individuals prepare for their exodus from the darkness of winter hibernacles. And silently filling the earthy spaces, transforming the sun's energy for the advancing hordes of voracious creatures, many green plants suddenly appear above the natural litter of last year. The exact time of spring's coming depends on the beholder since it is never recognized at the same moment by any two people; all of us entertain our own ideas, colored no doubt by pristine pleasant moments. For me it is the first day I am able to smell spring in the air as I ramble through the woods. Sweet, yet piquant, it is a full-flavored redolence of the land itself. I passed through decades of springtimes before learning that this most distinctive odor was the chemical by-product of latent soil bacteria, whose numbers soar with each drop of rain and each sunbeam.

By now I can clearly forecast the orderly individual appearances of many of the animals and plants since for years I have methodically recorded the first ribbon snake, wood frog, green tiger beetle, plantainleaf sedge spikelet, jumping mouse, water strider, or whatever new form for the year I have seen or heard on that day. Only rarely, though, have I been privileged to observe the actual annual emergence of an individual species.

One April day, while crossing the orchard, a slight movement on the ground caught my eye. To the right of my boot the earth was being heaved and humped. Just moments later a very muddy American toad pushed the damp soil aside, coming up at last to the surface after tunneling out of its winter hermitage. I would have expected it to blink awhile in the bright sunlight, to squat at the entrance of the small burrow for a time, to pull the fresh air back and forth between its vocal sac and lungs, to display some sign of heady response to its newly acquired unfettered existence. And in the toad's own way it did, as it immediately began jumping straight toward the shallow reaches of the distant pond, about a thousand toad hops away. I was sorry I couldn't follow it and watch it make that final leap into the mild water where it would join the toads already gathered there for their annual batrachian festival, all of them responding to the biological timeclock of toads. It would be pleasant to think it was returning to the pond because it recalled past good times there, but we are told that primarily man is given the gift of happy memories. I salute all toads, however, especially when I realize that they may live to make it through thirty-six of our winters into thirty-six springs.

Two years ago one May night, Milcey hurried into the house with the news that June bugs were coming up out of the ground everywhere back in the woods. As I returned there with her, she explained how at first she thought it had begun to rain, the drops of water hitting the dry, dead ground leaves. Once realizing it was not raining, she began to investigate and discovered that the large reddish beetles were the rainmakers as they crawled from the earth onto the woodland debris. As we walked down the path leading through the woods, we could hear those slight rustlings interrupted by a sudden buzzing whirr as one beetle would become airborne, climaxing three years of its development in that rich earth. We could tell when one was about to emerge since the leaves would be tilted. If we lifted the leafy cover, there would be a beetle parting the dirt and crawling out with its soft wings trailing. Soon, though, it would correctly fold its wings beneath its harder wing covers and find a stick or plant stem to hoist itself up on. Shortly thereafter it would make a brief trial flight or two and then suddenly zoom off over the moonlit white trilliums, over our heads, and up into the trees, joining the world of wings and leaving the strata of earthworms and snails behind. The next night many of these phototropic beetles were knocking themselves out against our lighted porch ceiling. We switched the lights off.

Then there was a hot May day that I remember well. I was thrashing through the criss-crossed jungle of fallen logs, brush and brambles, which seem to follow an ungrazed cut-over area, planning to check the nest of a chestnut-sided warbler. Instead, a colorful cecropia moth, newly issued from its winter cocoon, captured my attention. Several feet above the ground, clinging to a common elder stem, it was unhurriedly opening and closing its immense velvety wings. As I, the bystander, stood watching, I abruptly realized that the elegant moth was in imminent danger of never having the opportunity to use its wings, for slowly and smoothly moving up to the moth was a large pilot black snake. And then a most curious thing happened. The snake was so close and could easily have grasped the moth, but rather it chose to turn, easing itself down and away. I slowly let my breath out, I guess in relief, since I happened to prefer cecropia moths to huge snakes, but then I realized that the brief drama had not ended, because directly beneath the pile of brush I was balancing on a second black snake was gliding along heading for the same moth. It, too, climbed up the elder bush, carefully looked the moth over, and then withdrew, empty-jawed.

April this year, with all its restive weather, is quickening and cordial one day, only to withdraw the next. But yesterday was the kind of spring day that I await all winter long. An early morning fog veiled and softened the whole world of Sawdust as I gently shut the back door and stepped out with several hours of indulgence ahead of me. As I crossed the pasture, a winnowing Wilson snipe circled high overhead. Impossible to see it, of course, but the weird, mystical beats of its courtship flight were gloriously intensified in the moist air. We see and hear snipe well into June, which gives us reason to believe that they may nest on the farm, but so far we have never found their nest and it isn't because we haven't tried!

The spaced giant hills of the carmine and black Allegheny mound-building ants just outside the pasture were not opened so early in the morning, but I noted once again a bristly, tufted yellow, black, and white caterpillar hugging a tender young spear of grass sprouting from the anthill. Each year I find several of these larvae about the anthills very early in the spring, sometimes even on winter days. It appears to be an interesting adaptation, since the very first green spring blades of grass that shoot up in the spring do so on the fertile anthills, thus providing food for this caterpillar. I never knew what species it was until one April day I brought one home and let it complete its life cycle there. By June 1st it had developed into one of our most striking smaller moths, *Ctenucha virginica,* with its cobalt blue body, vivid orange head, black eyes and black wings edged with white.

Leaving the open spaces and dropping down into the valley,

I was intrigued by the noisy bursts of song of the Louisiana waterthrush as it deftly flew back and forth along the creek bed. Emerald clumps of wild leek plants spread over the dark earth; seeing them each spring often brings to mind my introduction to this *allium* fourteen years ago. What excitement when I first found these large, paired, lily-like-leaved plants, for I then thought they were orchids. For three uninformed years I faithfully checked them, waiting and watching for their blossoms. But, each year the leaves yellowed and withered away without a flower ever appearing. I know now that had I returned about the middle of July, long after the leaves had vanished, I would have discovered lovely umbels of white waxy blooms standing where the leaves had been.

A strange, shivering, soft sort of sound reached out to me as I picked my way through the wild flowers in the path. Puzzled, I stood still and began to scrutinize the nearby trees, hoping I would glimpse what it was before it sighted me. You cannot imagine my wonderment when I realized what I was hearing and seeing — a pair of wood ducks silhouetted against the sky as they sat on the branch of a large beech tree. The male, with his neck outstretched, looked more like a cormorant than a duck as he walked along the branch toward the preening female. Dropping down to a large cavity in an adjoining maple tree, he clung to the entrance, fluttering his wings and whinnying. Then he entered the hole, turned, came out again, and rejoined the female. This performance was repeated three times and, much to my interest, I watched the seemingly apathetic female. Her only response, if it can be called a response, was to ignore this gorgeous display of passion and pleading, as she ruffled and unruffled her feathers, not once even turning to look at him or the nesting site he was obviously attempting to show her. Once more he returned to her side and talked. By this time, I was muttering all sorts of things to myself, too, when suddenly he flew off and left her very much alone. Do you know what she did? As soon as he was out of sight, she looked at the hole in the maple, leaned down toward it, and then went and briefly slipped within. I watched for an hour; he never returned, but she was still sitting on the branch preening, waiting.

Green heron

Rabbit and young

Letter Ten: *Summer 1972*

IT IS JUNE, WITH BARN SWALLOWS, sun-warmed, sweetened, wild strawberries, and the subtle fragrance of wild grape blossoms. Soon the dark earth beneath the thickets of grapevines will be overlaid with tiny green scalloped discs as the grapevine flowers sift downward, so much fragile confetti. Clay towers of the land crayfishes appear in the floodplain or in the damper parts of the fields, some rising as high as five inches around their burrows. I used to wonder why this species of crayfish was named *Cambarus diogenes* since I could not visualize a crayfish with a lantern searching for an honest man. However, one night I looked up the ancient Greek philosopher and found that besides his renowned quest for integrity, Diogenes was supposed to have lived in a tub to demonstrate his austerity. Then I knew just how clever someone was because the land crayfish does indeed live in a little mud tub of water in the bottom of his deep burrow.

Toward the end of this month I can expect once again to hear the weak song of a very small cicada (*Okanagana rimosa*) which is found in our woods. We refer to it as our mystery bug because it is almost impossible to see and to our knowledge its life cycle is unknown. The eggs are supposed to be deposited in the tree branches; upon hatching, the larvae fall to the ground where they burrow down in search of succulent roots. How long they remain in the ground is uncertain but it could be many years since its close relative, the periodical cicada (alias seventeen-year locust), requires seventeen years to reach maturity.

While spring seems to be a time of hope for most of life, early summer means facing reality as so many forms cautiously venture forth. Slight fawns, newly fledged tottering birds, young foxes out of their dens, and many others like them may so easily and suddenly be separated from parents and life. It follows that at this time of the year the maternal instinct is so strong that even the most timid of creatures may be observed fighting for its young. Last week I watched a mother rabbit chase two crows away from her diminutive snub-nosed bunnies three times, and then on the same day I was literally charged by a ruffed grouse hen. She didn't bother with the broken-wing routine in defense of her chicks; instead, with head down and her back humped high, she ran straight for me uttering all sorts of threats. I retreated, not from fear, but rather in consideration of another mother's feelings. Down at our pond I sighted one more mother, a muskrat, having her problems, too. Five of her young ones were swimming around when suddenly two of them commenced to have what appeared to be quite a fight. The mother lost no time reaching them and breaking up the clinch, and as she proceeded to cuff one of the little ones with her paw, the other delinquent swam as speedily as it could in the opposite direction and thus avoided any punishment.

Summertime means spidertime, too. I am eagerly awaiting July and August because it is then that the orb-weaving spiders come into their own. Up until last summer I would have told you I could study anything in nature with pleasure, except spiders, parasitic worms, and poisonous snakes. I gazed with true respect and admiration at a lady I met who collected spiders in Mexico for an eastern museum. (Women school bus drivers impress me equally.) I walked around spiders if they were too big to be stepped on, I shuddered when I ran into their clinging webs stretched across a trail, and I yelled for Dick when I found a mammoth brown spider dancing around in the empty bathtub. To say I disliked them would be putting it mildly — I loathed them! Yet guilt accompanied the abhorrence since I realized what an important part they played in the natural world. Spiders were already on this planet when the very first vertebrate climbed out of the seas to live on land. As the early amphibia became less dependent on land, the presence of spiders helped them to change their diet from aquatic to terrestrial forms of life.

For years ten books on spiders collected dust on the top shelf of our reference library, but one rainy morning I pulled down one of those volumes and proceeded to read. Interested, at first in spite of myself, and then, as I read further, amazed and fascinated. Here was a highly specialized class with extraordinary instinctive powers exhibiting some of the most unique and bizarre characteristics to be found. And this could be observed right here in Ohio, in North America, on Sawdust, instead of being limited to the island of Mindora or some tropical rain forest in South America. So, fortified by a huge dose of curiosity, I began a summer of intense spider-watching. There are not enough pages to describe all that I was able to observe nor could I do justice if I tried, but I will say that I ended up with two hundred pages of scrawled notes and no preserved specimens. I am fairly confident that I did not watch anything that hadn't already been seen and described elsewhere, but it was the awe of what I was witnessing that kept me in a perpetual state of wonder.

It became apparent early in the study that to see spiders working I would do better watching them during the night hours since throughout the day most of them crouched in their retreats. I soon wished that flashlight batteries would outlast my patience but they never did, and about the seventh time I purchased another six-volt battery at the Thompson General Store, Maynard asked me if I had taken up burglarizing.

Spiders naturally fall into two family groups: hunting spiders which roam at will, stalking and capturing insects, and a second group which spins webs to trap insects. I chose more or less to concentrate on the secondary cobweb spiders since they remained in the same place and I could follow their daily activities. I first looked for examples of the main kinds of cobwebs: flat or sheet webs, irregular or netlike webs, round or orb webs, funnel webs, and triangular and special webs with loose bands of silk. It was a simple matter to locate all of the types, some found in the woods and many right in the yard.

A funnel-web spider, with its extensive sheet of very fine webbing and a funnel leading into its retreat, lived out its life right by our back door. And as the summer progressed, the spider's webs were a pretty sight early in the morning when they were covered with dew. By each of these ground webs a spider would be concealed within its silken tunnel, not running out unless an insect landed on its soft white web. I was interested that ants could climb over the webs without being attacked by the spider.

Tangled nets of silk stretched in every corner of the barn with brown soft-bodied spiders hanging upside down in the cobwebby maze. These spiders, of the family Theridiidae, are known as comb-footed spiders because they have a curious row of toothed bristles on the tarsus of their fourth pair of legs. These little combs are used to fling silk, often in almost a liquid state, over an insect. I saw the advantage of this one day when a paper wasp flew into a web. Many times smaller than the wasp, the spider still was able to subdue it without having to go too near until it had the wasp safely lassoed. Twenty-four hours later it was still feasting on its victim. Most spiders do not chew up their prey but liquefy the quarry's tissues so the fluid may be sucked.

Late one night I saw another theridiid *(Theridion redimitum)* tackle a click beetle four times her five-and-a-half-millimeter size. For two hours she worked to swathe the insect and then, with a fancy kind of engineering, she hoisted the beetle (still clicking) up to her home in a curled dock leaf with an elastic thread stronger than a similar-size strand of steel. I came to know this particular spider quite well; I even thought she was a delicate beauty. A few days later, after the beetle episode, on August 16th between midnight and six-thirty in the morning, within the same dock leaf, she spun a light bluish-green egg sac. For fifteen days she guarded her egg-cocoon as it hung in a small mesh of threads. I do not believe she ever left it to eat since she stood guard over her newly hatched spiderlings. What finally happened to them all I do not know for I found the dock leaf on the ground — empty.

There is just one species *(Hyptiotes cavatus)* that spins a triangular web here in the east. After reading of this unusual web, I began searching and to my pleasure found it in the woods the first night out. There were many of them stretched vertically between twigs of dead saplings, some low to the ground, some as high as ten feet. And I was ashamed to realize that I had undoubtedly walked past hundreds of them through the years, failing to notice something so geometrically different among spider webs. The web is a sector of a circle, about a sixth of it, the same shape as a piece of cut pie. Viscid lines go between the four radii which are attached together to a single line at the apex. The minute spider sits on that line up against the branch and keeps the web very taut by holding the line fast with its claws. If you stand there long enough eventually you will get to see an ingenious snare sprung into action. When a gnat or midge lands, the spider instantly releases the web tension and collapses the bands around the insect. She then tightens it again and loosens it once more until she hurries out after the trapped bug.

Each night of wandering through the woods or just sitting by one web for hours turned up something new for me, sometimes rather startling. Such as the night I watched a small male spider courting a larger female. Always approaching carefully and slowly, he finally met her, only to end up losing a leg and almost his life. He dropped from sight but she hung there sucking the juice from the thin limb she had seized. One would think that the male would have learned a lesson, but instead he returned once again to her side. But she seemed to have lost interest in him; she was dining. I observed two species of damselflies, *Ischnura posita* and *I. verticalis,* return each night to the same resting place for a week. They slept with folded wings, not moving until the sun warmed their dew-covered bodies the next morning. I saw the first dew drops appear on the tips of grass and then roll down like cold tears as the night progressed. With the dark and dampness, slugs began to appear on the ground and the herbage, and everywhere daddy-long-legs hunted for food. One evening, just as my watch showed midnight, I saw a daddy-long-legs floating to the earth on a bit of Canadian thistle fluff.

At three-thirty-five one warm night, as I was sitting with a spider and her web, a nearby grasshopper *(Conocephalus brevipennis)* began to moult, pulling itself slowly out of its old skin where it then hung with curled antennae, small folded wings, and legs straight out. By five-ten that morning it was able to move away and five minutes later a tree cricket was eating the cast skin left behind by the grasshopper. I learned that katydids and black-billed cuckoos called all night long. I often saw spiders pull down yesterday's orb webs, looking so much like ladies taking their laundry down from the clotheslines. But the spiders rolled up the old silk and chewed on it before they threw it to the ground.

Just as dawn begins the first cardinal sings; many of the deft orb-wearing spiders begin swiftly to fashion their daily web. It takes them only about forty-five minutes to complete a new web and the freshly spun silken webs, as they gently waft back and forth, are probably one of nature's supreme contributions to beauty on this earth. Another ideal time to watch these Rumpelstiltskins spin is just at dusk. The precise design of the orb-weaving spider web differs with each genus, and I was soon able to distinguish the various fixed patterns, whether it was a miniature web of a spiderling or that of an adult.

I wanted to see a spider spin her cocoon and lay her eggs. Night after night I checked all of my very fat *Argiopes* but I managed to see only one working on her cocoon. They seemed to wait until I left to climb down from their webs and find a suitable plant on which to fasten their egg-sac. The female I did succeed in watching a little had left her web about five o'clock but I did not find where she had gone until two-thirty in the morning. By then the cocoon was already about the size and color of a small wet hickory nut, and she was merely going around and around the sac adding more silk. Though her movements were slow and she seemed tired, she worked continually and then about three o'clock she began pulling the aster leaves down around it, fastening them to the cocoon with more silk. A strong wind sprang up with distant rumblings and flashings and by four o'clock it was pouring rain, but this didn't delay her; she kept on concealing and securing her gift to the future. Five o'clock came, I fed Blackie when he thundered into the barn, and I nodded sleepily to a toad which had taken shelter in the barn too, and then I checked the spider once more. She was barely able to lift herself up as she worked. I was weary and drenched by that time also, so I headed for the house. But I was sorry that I hadn't remained to see what followed, because somehow she retraced her path to her old web, which was fifteen feet away. Considering the thousands of times she went up and down, backward and forward, in that long night, it seemed a prodigious achievement. In spite of her eight eyes, she could not have seen it because spiders are very nearsighted. At eleven o'clock that morning she pulled down her used web with painfully slow movements, almost losing her hold at times. I never saw her again.

Summer nights are full of intrigue and somehow the words of Holland, written sixty-nine years ago in his *Moth Book,* seem very apt at three-thirty in the morning in a darkened, still woodland:

When the moon shall have faded out from the sky, and the sun shall shine at noonday a dull cherry-red, and the seas shall be frozen over, and the ice-cap shall have crept downward to the equator from either pole, and no keels shall cut the waters, nor wheels turn in mills, when all cities shall have long been dead and crumbled into dust, and all life shall be on the very last verge of extinction on this globe; then, on a bit of lichen, growing on the bald rocks beside the eternal snows of Panama, shall be seated a tiny insect, preening its antennae in the glow of the worn-out sun, representing the sole survivor of animal life on this our earth, — a melancholy "bug."

Cottontail rabbit

Chicory

LETTER ELEVEN: *Fall 1972*

THIS MORNING AS I STARTED OUT, the hushed, dimmed world seemed to be sleeping in; not even a wayward cricket was chirping. It had been cold last night and I imagined everything was joining me in anticipating the sunrise, though I suddenly realized that millions of eyes on Sawdust must be turned toward the treasured dawn each day, while I, with the vision and mind to value it, too frequently slept through one of the world's most spectacular events. But not today, because I hastened toward Tupelo Hill for the express purpose of seeing the sun's first slanted rays light up the fiery red leaves of the tupelo trees growing there.

The darkness and silence made it simpler to hurry since there were no distracting unknown bird calls and the various red, orange, blue, white, or green berries dangling on the many plants lining the trail were familiar colorful ornaments as the flashlight beam momentarily illuminated them. I did pause at the pond's edge and was startled as a kingfisher flew in, landing on the crooked willow stub next to me. What it was doing up so early puzzled me; surely they do not hunt for food in the darkness. Perhaps it was migrating and chose to drop down there. Half an hour later found me at the desired vantage spot settling down with my thermos of hot coffee and my thoughts. The melancholic, silvery cry of a killdeer sliced the early morning air followed by the plaintive, sweet, and hesitant notes of a small scattered flock of bluebirds. I blamed my shivers of sadness on autumn because those same songs in March would elate me.

A movement below, and my coffee cup was fast exchanged for binoculars. A red fox, hunting in the grassy, weedy hollow, entertained me for some time. Acting more like a cat, it would suddenly leap up, twist sidewise, and then pounce so nimbly. Apparently it missed its prey a few times but finally, after being successful, vigorously waved its bushy tail. I had difficulty determining through the glasses what it had caught, but its prey looked like a chunky meadow vole. Since these stubby-tailed rodents weigh as much as two-and-a-half ounces, the fox would have had at least one more good gulp to conclude the night's hunting.

Forever haunting me is the memory of two sickened meadow voles I once watched in one of our fields. They were spinning fast, around and around and around, as though an invisible record turntable supported them. They were still revolving as I turned away in horror. I felt a personal responsibility for their plight because we had permitted a young neighbor to plant that acreage in pickles and had not thought to tell him we did not want it sprayed. What he used for a poison spray or what quantities he used we will never know but many mice died; the barred owl that hunted that stretch became so ill that it allowed us to pick it up from the ground before it died there. That field was an entomological desert for three years thereafter. We were glad we had not picked or eaten any of his cucumbers and we speculated about the folk who bought the bottled pickles.

But I have digressed far from this morning. I didn't mind if a fox killed a meadow vole, for the world would still contain meadow voles, foxes, you, and me. And sunrises! I was not disappointed; each dew-moistened, crimson leaf deepened with the early morning sunrays. The quality of the dawn light, unlike any other time of the day, was the ingredient needed to complete the flaring beauty of autumn tupelos. Perhaps to you this tree is known as blackgum or sourgum.

Long ago, cattle grazed on Tupelo Hill but now groundhogs, grasshoppers, deer, rabbits, mice, slugs, and caterpillars chew away, unmolested by us. Here the wild strawberries ripen first and it is the only place on Sawdust that the arrow-leaved violet (*V. sagittata*) grows. It is also home for a colony of the rare and local regal fritillary butterflies. As I sat there on Tupelo Hill, with the sun climbing ever higher and warming my back, honey bees began to appear on the heavy heads of goldenrod. As they energetically nuzzled the bright blossoms, I watched them with such appreciation; every day I use their honey and almost every night I light the golden beeswax candles that Dick makes for me from the capping wax left after extracting the honey. The last time he brought in thirty-six tall candles from his barn workshop! No candle burns with a steadier gleam or lasts as long. As we eat I see untold thousands of worn little wings fanning the candle flames whereas Dick is more accurate: he told me it took roughly one-and-a-quarter million bee flights to produce the wax for the latest bundle of candles.

My eyes lazily followed the white clumps of clouds above.

Barely moving, poised against the azure sky, they held their shapes for long periods. Porpoises, puppies, ant-eaters, ponies, seashores, mountains, Gibson girls, eagles, and profiled faces — all were there, but as the time passed, so did they. And then a distant gunshot shattered the morning's calm.

Probably I have met more hunters up on Tupelo Hill than any other place on Sawdust since it is so simple for them to slink in there, a mile away from the house. I've missed the protection of Lisa, our St. Bernard, this year, for the men used to leave without a debate when they watched me struggling to hold onto her collar with my two hands as she plunged toward them. Just once I freed her and she almost knocked the hunter to the ground as she attempted to retrieve the grouse in his hunting coat. The varied excuses such men give for being on posted property would fill several pages by now, but the top honors for stupidity would go to the hunter who said, "I didn't think anyone owned this." Perhaps I wouldn't be bitter against such men if I hadn't come up over a rise one day only to see a hunter aiming a shotgun right at me.

The gap between hunters and sportsmen becomes more obvious with each trespasser. The hunter is not capable of realizing that many of us find watching the living animal intensely interesting and that we are happy to see it move away, still very much alive. The hunter fails to honor the printed notice on his hunting license: *"You must have permission to hunt on private property."* If this law were strictly observed and enforced, the increase of all wildlife in Ohio would be tremendous, and the surplus on the protected farms and tracts of land would quickly spread out to adjoining areas where the owner welcomes hunting. Some animals might even become pest species. I am indebted, however, to the sportsman since I am well aware of the vast tracts of wild land that are being preserved by him and for him. While he may annihilate the game there, pretty much everything else in the natural world remains intact. The emerald carpets of moss are just as soft, the dragonflies are just as brilliant, and the bird songs are just as sweet on a state hunting ground as in a state park.

The moral obligation so many feel toward all wildlife is a sobering burden. On the frontier, the forests and swamps represented problem areas and much work; they were the home of hostile Indians and of wild animals against which the settler did not have any sophisticated means of defense. And to make the land suitable for agriculture, forests and wet lands had to be adapted. Today, the situation is reversed. The remnants of the original forests and swamps are precious jewels surrounded by a sea of agriculture and urban mediocrity. The situation has changed drastically but the attitudes of many people have not. This is the greatest challenge to the educational endeavors of museums and schools: to convince people that nature's heartbeat is in truth their own — a Herculean task.

Leaving Tupelo Hill for home, I chose to take the shady trail of hemlocks along the creek. I accompanied one small yellow leaf as it floated down the creek, watching it drift between sedge beds, round a slippery rock, lightly touch the partly submerged gnarled root of a tree, cross a pool sideways, bump down a riffle, until it finally became one of a number of leaves wedged against a fallen branch. A great blue heron clumsily arose ahead of me and from the tone of its squawks, it was either scared or angry for having been disturbed while the fishing was so fine. I re-entered the world of brilliant sunshine as I approached the barnyard. Passing a browned clump of chicory plants, I thought how I had studied them for a few hours last month. The showy masses of gay blue blossoms of this weed are a special bright spot in anyone's morning on the journey along our rural roadsides.

Since I had never simply sat and watched a flower unfold, I decided to do so and chose a chicory. At midnight I could tell which blossom would be opening that morning and by two o'clock the blue of the rays was obvious. But it wasn't until six-fifteen that the blue rays lengthened and appeared distinct, although still closed. By six-fifty the rays proceeded to open and by seven-ten I was able to see the white center deep within the partially opened flower head. At eight-ten the blossom was an inch across with the square serrated tips of the petalled rays now visible. It then took the long, deep blue stigmas twenty-five minutes to emerge and separate, ready for the bumblebee which landed on the blossom at precisely eight-thirty-five. Less than four hours later, the flower had faded and closed forever.

We were fully prepared for leaking roofs, uninsulated walls, uneven floors, ants, basement snakes, mice, and hibernating wasps when we signed the papers for our tiny farmhouse on Sawdust; we had ascertained that the lovely fieldstone fireplace burned well and that the water supply was excellent. But no one had ever mentioned to us that we were also purchasing an echo. Not just an ordinary echo, but one that answered three times! I do not recall who first discovered it — the children or the dog — as they played in front of the house, but it has been a fanciful thing through the years. Can you imagine a more appealing way to end a day than to hear taps being echoed three times? So many guests have shouted out their "hel-loooo"s and been enchanted as they listened to the replies. As I type this, I realize no one has ever called out "goodbye" to the echo, not even Rick when he left for Korea or Milcey when she moved to Wyoming. But I shall, the day I must leave the magic world of Sawdust.

Wild grape

LETTER TWELVE: *Winter 1972*

No WIND WAS THERE TO DISTURB the falling white flakes. They simply steadily continued moving downward, and no matter where I looked, all I could see were more flakes coming toward me: silent snowflakes, landing gently, wreathing the hemlocks with leis of the purest white blossoms. A thick, white storm but a kindly one and ideal to be out in, since it was not very cold. I had a pruning saw and clippers with me to demolish grapevines. While we welcome grapevine tangles in many places, we do attempt to keep them out of the hemlock trees. Hence, I was working at the edge of Sawdust's largest grove of hemlocks, with piles of snow breaking loose and spraying down the back of my neck, as I untangled, cut, and wrenched the vines, hoping my strength would undo the vigorous growth of last summer.

The shredded, gray, papery remains of a previously globular hornet nest still hung on one of the hemlock branches. Its tiered interior, once so meticulously assembled, and full of life, was now torn and empty except for the snow filling up each small six-sided cell.

It is surprising how promptly, after the hornets have deserted the large nest in the fall, the nests are opened and the abandoned larvae are eaten. I have always wondered what animal or bird takes advantage of this situation to assail these paper vaults. A similar thing happens to the underground paper nests of yellow jackets because I have frequently found layers of their comb scattered on the ground alongside a scooped-out hollow, following the first killing frost. Occasionally in the winter, I will come upon a hibernating white-faced hornet queen sheltered within a decaying log, but never have I cupped one in my hand to see if she will respond to its warmth.

Much of particular interest to us has been observed in this hemlock grove. The magnolia warbler and the solitary vireo have each nested here as well as the Canada warbler on the steep bank below. Screaming bluejays once drew my attention to the only long-eared owl ever seen on Sawdust, as it sat in one of the hemlocks. There is a fox den at the far end of the grove. For years the hay-scented fern flourished on the edges and the frail spidery blossoms of the Indian cucumber-root were bright pins amidst the brown carpet of hemlock needles but, with changing light conditions, these plants are dwindling. In contrast, there is a bird or pin cherry tree *(Prunus pensylvanica)* growing up between the hemlock trees to record size for Sawdust and perhaps the state as well. This species of cherry is confined to the northeastern counties here in Ohio; it is a nice addition to our woody flora since it has such showy white flowers in the spring, followed by light red fruit.

As I continued my guerrilla activities in that snowclad microcosm, it seemed to me that the rest of the world had temporarily departed since no sounds, except my own, desecrated the stillness. I found myself listening for a faraway car or cow, a chipping cardinal — just any noise. Finding none, I resumed working with a complacent smile.

We have always been grateful that the lumbermen spared this grove of hemlocks when our place was logged out. Since the cutting took place before we purchased the property, we never understood why. I like to think the previous owners thought it was too lovely a spot to spoil, whereas practical Dick thinks it did not pay the lumbermen to cut it. Our nine sawdust piles are a mute testimonial to the amount of timber that must have been removed.

Until we moved out here and Harley Valentine began to build our barn, I never realized how wood varied. As he worked, he would talk about the various kinds of wood and lumber. "Sweet wood, like hickory or maple, burns good . . . osage orange sparks right through the screen . . . butternut puts it out." "If you turn lilac wood on a lathe, it is blue like the blossoms . . . sumac wood is the prettiest of all." "Cottonwood — the water flies when you saw it . . . but you should smell sassafras when that goes through the maple syrup on basswood chips." "Tulip is the best white wood, all clear."

Thinking of this massive stand of green conifers, more than a mile away, is enough to draw any one of us out of the house at any season of the year. It is the halfway mark on our "loop trail" and as such is visited frequently. One evening last week Dick left after dinner for a committee meeting in town; I was alone. But a full moon was rising, the snow held a firm crust, and there were my snowshoes hanging in the mud room. The thought of standing beneath those hemlocks, with the moonlight shining through them onto the snow, was just too tempting. I knew the bitter cold would match the brightness of the night and I also knew it was too far for the time I had; nevertheless, I recklessly fastened on my bear paws and carefully began plodding toward the hemlock grove: through the big woods, where the branches above were cracking like rifle shots with the winter's iciness, then out to Tupelo Hill. Passing the dried heads of tall flat-topped asters, goldenrods, and mountain-mint, I paused to crumble and sniff one of the mint's pungent old flowers, and a tiny bit of midsummer briefly returned. Everything was visible on the moon-flooded hillside and I was sorry I had needlessly burdened myself with a six-volt flashlight. I could see the unharvested corn stalks with the heavy ears dropping, standing in the field to the right of Tupelo Hill. From the worn game trails leading into it, it was evident that it has been a fine source of food for the wildlife on Sawdust. Throughout the winter, Dick keeps ears of corn strung up outside the barn, which attract many fox squirrels. It has always interested us that the squirrels will first eat out the germ of the kernel, letting the rest just fall to the ground. Ordinarily, I would detour to the corn field and gather up some ears of corn to scatter in the hemlock and down in the floodplain, but there was no time. I saw where a fox had been trailing a rabbit, but apparently the fox had surprised a quail and had eaten that instead.

So on I stamped, leaving my patterned tracks behind, and thoroughly enjoying myself when, suddenly, I almost panicked and my wild isolation became a frightful thing. Moments before I had been pitying all the folk attending the committee meeting, but at that point I envied them in their snug little conference room. Because coming toward me was a pack of wild dogs — the only thing I am truly afraid of in our woods. This pack, comprising two large German shepherds, a black chow, and a white collie-like mongrel, has ravaged the livestock and game in our township for more than a year. Because nearly everyone shoots at them on sight, the dogs usually melt out of sight the minute they see a person. But I had seen how they circled and leapt up at our horse in the pasture one early morning. I wondered if they would dare to attack me when they sensed my fear, which was intensified by my utter defenselessness as I balanced there on snowshoes. With my heart racing as rapidly as they were coming, I simply stood and awaited them; there was nothing else I could do. But one of them abruptly realized there was a human being just ahead of them. Instantly veering, they changed their course and were soon gone.

I slowly pulled myself together and went on to the hemlocks. And they were lovely as the moonlight filtered through their branches! Facing a long journey home, I did not linger too long. Crossing the creek below the grove, I was startled that I could still hear water moving restlessly through a pocket in the ice. As I moved along the valley floor, passing black stationary tree trunks which soared into a profusion of silhouetted branches, I thought how we go to so much effort to ornament our Christmas trees, until they are so grandly gaudy. I decided that if I were able, I would instead carve life-size from wood and then paint many tiny, black-capped chickadees and golden-crowned kinglets, a few cardinals, white-winged crossbills, one diminutive brown creeper, and a bluejay or two, plus several goldfinches in their winter plumage. These I would place on a hemlock tree filled with its natural cones. Next, I would use nothing but the old-fashioned wax candles in their little metal holders that used to decorate and light the Christmas trees of my childhood. Such starlit reverie lasted until I came up to the barnyard and saw the lights of home.

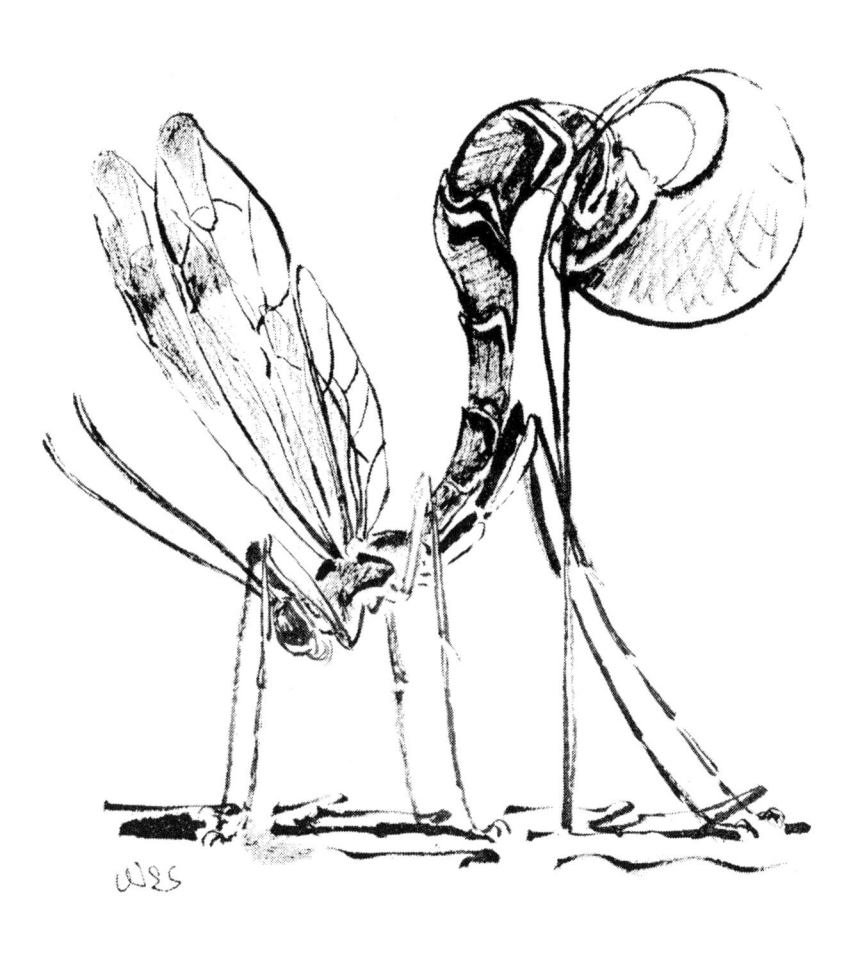

Ichneuman fly

*Spring buds; clockwise from the upper left:
dogwood, tulip, hickory, red maple*

LETTER THIRTEEN: *Spring 1973*

THAT SPECIAL MORNING COMES AT LAST, when I open the back door and soft sweet air glides in past me, buoying up my winter-sagged spirits as nothing else can. Is it my spring-excited imagination, or do the crowing roosters honestly sound giddy as they indulge in cross-talk between coops? No need for a heavy, wearisome jacket or mittens as I start down the long driveway to get the morning paper. Sawdust suddenly gives me the feeling that everywhere creatures are going somewhere. Cardinals, perched high, are emphatically whistling, while English sparrows scatter from mud puddles, where they had been splashing and screeching so insistently at one another. My halcyon mood even includes those sparrows — after all, they are a part of Sawdust. Rivulets of dirty water are beginning to trickle down the field, loosening the uneven, hard ridges of snow piled for so long along the driveway. This undermining of winter's work cannot happen soon enough, as far as I am concerned; I cheer the mud puddles on! (But the morning that I find the first pinkish, stranded earthworms in one of these pools, I will know that spring has truly come.) I search the blue sky for streaming flocks of blackbirds and listen for a scolding robin or two. Instead, I see a lone sparrow hawk, poised on a telephone wire, ready to drop momentarily should it sight a mouse. Even though I stand absolutely still, my presence seems to disturb the small trim falcon, and it is off across the field in swift easy flight.

Already the honey bees are out and flying, swarming around the scratch feed at the bird feeders. Today they will probably be able to return to the bee hives, but just two weeks ago they left the hives, encouraged by a warming sun, only to meet cold air and drop by the hundreds into the snow banks. This seems to happen early each year, and I am always interested how quickly the black-capped chickadees and tufted titmice discover this bonanza of fresh food. Since they eat only the head and thorax of bees, multitudes of yellow-and-black-striped abdomens are left lying on the snow. I have frequently checked the wild-bee trees when this takes place in our bee yard, but only rarely have bees from those trees been found to leave their combs in such a manner. Perhaps the bee tree is better insulated than the man-made hive body. The very first good natural food source for the bees will be the yellowish green blossoms on our silver maple trees. If the weather is favorable and these precious blooms are amply pollinated, the mature seeds are excellent early food for chipmunks, squirrels, and mice; even the hungry muskrats leave the pond and come up to gather mouthfuls of the fallen green-winged seeds.

I am more aware at this time of the year than any other of the natural order that appears to exist all about me. Providential nature! The aspen buds swell early and there, sitting up among the aspen's knobby twigs, is a ruffed grouse filling its crop with the juicy buds. A raccoon, coming out of hibernation, is caught and killed by a couple of dogs, but almost immediately I find five large, flattened carrion beetles crawling over the lifeless coon's body — repulsive, perhaps, but necessary. Red maples are bright with their buds and blossoms and, so, all through the woodland, red and fox squirrels are daintily nipping off these crimson delicacies. The semi-aquatic ribbon snake comes out of hibernation ahead of most of the snakes, but there are untold numbers of tiny spring peepers, chorus frogs, and red-spotted newts gathered together for the snake to stalk. Earthworms work their way up in the soil to be found, perhaps, by the long, sensitive, probing bill of the newly arrived woodcock. Down in the field, about the time life in the anthills begins to stir once again, the migrating flickers are passing through; it is not unusual to see a dozen or more mounds, each with a flicker pecking away on its crest, finding a fast and easy meal. Small queens of the solitary bees emerge from their underground burrows just in time to pollinate the ephemeral spring beauties and hepaticas. Then, as though held in reserve for the time when most of the other kinds of berries are gone, the hard seed coverings of the staghorn sumac commence to soften and swell so that many species of birds may feast on the sturdy, bright, now-ripened clusters. Robins, bluebirds, chickadees, ruffed grouse, bluejays, crows, red-winged blackbirds, starlings, scarlet tanagers, catbirds, brown thrashers, hermit and Swainson's thrushes, veeries, purple finches, flickers, downy and hairy woodpeckers and even the pileated have all been observed here eating the fruit, until it is entirely consumed sometime in May.

How we value our sumacs on Sawdust! Not simply because they are natural and colorful bird feeders, but their dazzling, massive, greenish-white flower heads furnish much nectar for the bees at a time in the summer when not much else is blooming. The lush, tropical-looking foliage of the sumac transforms any place it grows, whether in the open or dipping over an ancient pigpen or corncrib, into an artistic triumph. And then visualize these graceful clumps in pennants waving against the azure sky. What more could a person ask from one species of tree? If you truly desire more, the sumac will oblige: its red velour berries make a pleasant-tasting tea; its wood has the loveliest color and most striking grain of any for turning on a wood lathe; its bark and leaves are a rich source of tannin; its twigs furnish good browse for deer and rabbits.

Our farmyard has an ever-changing parade of animals but usually there is at least one skunk or opossum living beneath a shed or the porch. Presently we have a big old opossum that is constantly startling one of us when we reach in to gather the eggs, since it appears to find a nest box a comfortable place in which to sleep. No chickens have been finalized by it and if it eats some eggs before it snoozes, we do not mind. After all, opossums could perhaps have eaten the eggs of Diatrymas sixty million years ago and any species that could have waddled from that world, virtually unchanged, into ours, just has to be more astute than it appears, and deserving of some of our chickens' eggs. Our battle-scarred, frost-bitten opossum looks and acts so defenseless. The other evening a skunk challenged its possession of the chicken coop, but instead of yielding, the opossum stood its ground, facing the skunk, with its imbecilic grin and jet black eyes wide open. All the woes of that opossum were hastily compounded when the skunk ejected pungent fluid.

When I think how we share Sawdust with many animals such as the raccoon, skunk, opossum, fox, weasel, squirrel, mink, beaver, and deer, I cannot help but wonder about the very earliest settlers here in Trumbull Township. Their written accounts tell of marauding bears, wolves, and wildcats and the first recorded township death was Leonard Blackmer, who died in 1819 "from the effects sustained in his efforts to capture a big elk singlehanded."

As the chartreuse new leaves of the willows begin to show, we will be watching for the emerging caterpillar of a red-spotted purple butterfly, from its hibernaculum on the end of one of the willow branches. This tiny tube, closely resembling a terminal tree bud, was made last fall by the caterpillar by rolling itself up in a willow leaf. It has been deluged with rain and sleet, covered with snow, frosted, frozen, and thawed but the golden thread of life is durable. Upon leaving its snug winter retreat, the half-grown caterpillar will continue eating willow leaves until it is ready to pupate. We consider these hibernacula to be one of the rare finds on Sawdust; it is amazing how many willows can be examined before one is discovered that is being used by the caterpillar of the red-spotted purple. To be able to study their life history more completely, we decided to experiment with a method that Dick refers to as "butterfly farming." He built cages of screen wire around the food plants (willow) and then placed the adult butterflies within. Minute eggs were laid on the tips of the willow leaves. Since the larvae of the red-spotted purple are cannibalistic, ordinarily only one egg is laid on each leaf, but occasionally two were found together. The eggs measured approximately one millimeter in diameter, necessitating the use of a microscope to see the delicate sculpturing on the surface of the egg. Butterfly eggs generally are very beautiful, with varying colors and shapes. Some are round, some barrel-shaped or hemispherical with cross lines or ribbed or rugose surfaces. I suppose a butterfly egg, a twenty-fifth of an inch in diameter, may seem absolutely insignificant compared to the problems we face each day, but, as Victor Hugo once put it, "There are prodigious relations between beings and things; and in this inexhaustible total, from the flea to the sun, nothing despises the other, for all have need of each other."

Since spring has a way of singing the same happy melody each year, I know that soon my days will be brightened by many things: the first song of the Louisiana waterthrush or a noble tiger swallowtail butterfly sailing overhead as I walk up the valley; conversational wood frogs; mounds of long-stemmed blue violets or buttery marsh marigolds; the odor of the trailing arbutus enjoyed one more time; slender catkins on the poplars blowing in the wind; a brown thrasher singing as I hang out freshly washed blankets; Baltimore orioles and apple blossoms; carpets of pale bluets covering the pasture. But if the notes of the bluebirds this year in Ohio seem to be sadder for all of us, it is because we are all remembering Dr. Mirian Bell, Ohio's First Bluebird Lady.

And then will come the day when Dick decides it is safe to open wide the doors of the winter houses of the guineas and ducks. Somehow, their noisy, wild scrambling reflects our own thoughts of spring.

Flowers of the shadbush

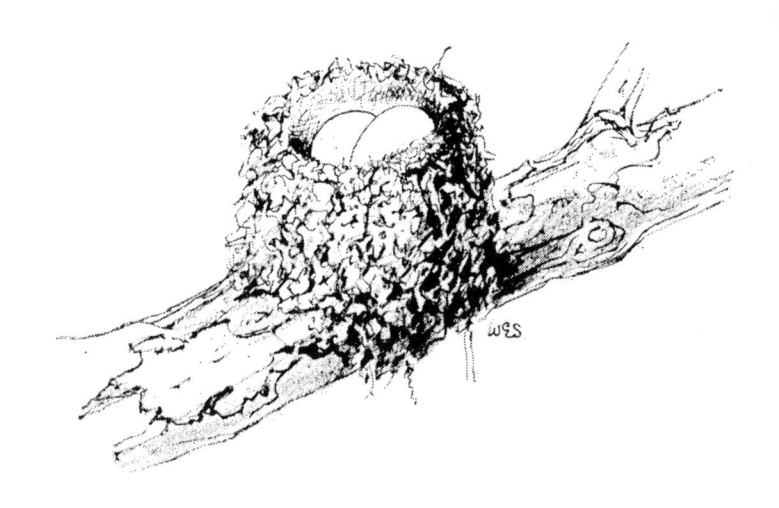

Hummingbird nest

LETTER FOURTEEN: *Summer 1973*

JUNE 11TH. To experience the awakening each day of a summer woodland is to be able to interpret it in a better way, and no matter how many mornings I enter that hushed, murkily lit, beguiling world, it is with that wondrous expectant feeling that all nature lovers share and understand. This morning I hoped to see how early a female ruby-throated hummingbird would leave her nest, so I proceeded fairly quickly down to the bank of Penny Creek, where I had found a low nest. I did pause once to watch some Crecropia moths. These pre-dawn phantoms, lightly brushing against the branches, proved to be two males drawn to a waiting female moth. Completely disregarding the flashlight beam and me, the male moths fluttered about the low limb the female Cecropia was clinging to, until one of the males found her.

When I reached the creek, a furtive check with the flashlight showed that the hummingbird was still on her nest, so I settled down to enjoy the swelling, vibrant chorus of bird songs. Though it was warm, I wore a light pair of gloves to discourage mosquitoes. Twenty feet above me was a nest of a downy woodpecker; however, the young birds had not yet begun their incessant daytime screeching from within the hollowed-out nest. Because these, as well as nestling hairy woodpeckers, are so noisy for at least two weeks before leaving their nesting cavities, it is surprising to me they are not all annihilated by predators. The perfectly round entrance that the downy woodpecker fashions is unique — one would think a compass had been used. I observed this particular nest being chiseled out. The downy's muffled pounding deep within could be heard, then shortly it would appear at the entrance to spit out the wood chips.

How differently the hummingbird worked as she constructed her tiny nest, a seamstress as compared to a carpenter. I would see her searching along the shale bank where spiderwebs stretched between tangles of exposed tree roots, rocks, and branches. Into these pockets she would move, hovering there, carefully picking out the sticky strands — flying backwards and quickly darting to another spot — until she had a number of them in her needle-like bill, and then up to her nest. Reddish bud scales of the beech tree were fastened to the nest with these cobwebs and then she covered the bud scales with small gray curls of lichen. One female I watched failed to add this lichen veneer to her nest; consequently, the nest was rather conspicuous on the gray supporting beech limb. Possibly that was why it was torn apart and robbed of its eggs four days after she had begun incubating. Unlike the young downy woodpeckers which snuggle down on wood fragments, nestling hummingbirds have almost a velvet cushion made of plant down. Hummingbird nests are easily discovered if one spends some time during the last two weeks in May along a wooded creek, since the female hummer pays little attention to anything or anyone while she is busy gathering nesting materials. She may squeak at you a few times, but that only helps to alert you to the fact she has a nest nearby. There are four hummingbird nestings. These blackbirds move into the creek bottom to feed on minnows trapped in waning pools about the same time the young hummingbirds are developing. The nestlings of the wood pewee, the Acadian flycatcher, and the blue gray gnatcatcher are also subject to the grackle's attack. I watched them raiding a gnatcatcher's nest one day, and nothing was more pitiful that afternoon than to see those two tiny gray sprites futilely trying to drive the grackles away. The Acadian flycatchers attempt to nest a second time and, by the time the young are hatched, the grackles have disappeared from along the creek and so some of these nestlings are fledged.

I never see a male around any of the hummingbird nests, but I am intrigued by what an attentive mate the male Acadian flycatcher is. It is an insignificant thing to mention, and I will probably be accused of anthropomorphism for doing so, yet it was touching to observe. One evening as darkness was climbing up the wall of the valley, a male Acadian flycatcher flew down to his mate on her nest. Perching on the side of the nest, he leaned over the brooding female to stroke and smooth her feathers with his bill, softly twittering the whole time. And then he flew to his nighttime roost.

It seemed to me this morning, as I quietly sat there in the woods, that I could sense the approaching daylight before I could see it. A faint breeze began to stir the calm morning air while vague forms eased their way into sight, and overhead the stars gradually dimmed. I watched three striped woodsnails (*Anguis-*

pira alternata), whose homeplace I was sharing, slowly moving downward on the log, returning to their daytime retreat beneath the loosened bark. While the snails will hide from bright sunlight, the sun's warming rays will draw out another occupant of this pile of logs — the five-lined skink, northeastern Ohio's only lizard. No time for lonely thoughts as the minutes melted away on such a faultless June morning; even the crested flycatcher chose to sing. How puzzled I was the first time I heard its dawn song, since I had known only its loud calls before.

I was sitting in the part of Sawdust that we call "Vireo Valley." Red-eyed vireos and yellow-throated vireos add musically, with their persistent songs, to the summer valley, and occasionally the solitary vireos and white-eyed vireos have sung and nested along its banks, too. The latter species, a very rare nesting bird for Ashtabula County, chose to nest in the biggest tangle of grapevines and witch-hazels on one of the steepest banks of the ravine, and while finding the nest took many hours and much luck, photographing it was the real challenge. The view camera had to be held in place with ropes on the vertical bank and Dick was obliged to work with only one hand, since the other was needed for hanging on. To complicate things further, a thunderstorm was threatening. Fortunately, the bird was very cooperative and Dick managed to get one picture before the deluge came. As the white-eyed vireo slipped back on her nest, Dick threw his raincoat over the camera and scrambled up the bank to the shelter of a large hemlock.

My watch read five-ten in the morning when the hummingbird abruptly left her nest with its two eggs. She flew up to a nearby bare perch, where she sat preening herself with her long bill and a foot. And then she was gone. I left, too.

Empty spaces were scarce, as I carefully walked up the floodplain through the profusion of plants. The light-green spore cases on the fertile erect stem of the rattlesnake fern reached above my ankles, while the flowering hellebores and tall meadow-rues were almost shoulder high. Fragrant clusters of bloom covered a sprawling multi-flora rose clump and, overhead, purplish wedge-shaped new samaras crowded the white ash leaflets. Where it was more open, Oswego-tea or been-balm formed large patches, and in the shadier sections the touch-me-nots were thriving. Later on, in July, when these two species are blooming, they will frequently be visited by the hummingbirds in search of nectar. Nature's jewelry is on display when a shaft of sunlight illuminates an emerald-backed hummingbird poised in front of the vivid orange pendulous blossom of a spotted touch-me-not.

Black cohosh *(Cimicifuga racemosa)* plants were scattered throughout the floodplain too and by the first week in July their elongated racemes will rise above most vegetation. I have found this black cohosh to be a food plant for the larvae of the spring azure butterfly. These caterpillars chew into the rounded flower buds, and as the blooms open gradually up the stem, so do the larvae progress. By the time the plant has finished blooming (the end of July) there is sometimes a fat greenish-white caterpillar curled around a single bud at the tip of the raceme. The caterpillars I watched then formed greenish pupae, which turned brown as they hardened and dried. A caterpillar was well camouflaged as it lived among the buds and flowers of the plant, but its presence was often betrayed by attending black ants running up and down the flowering stem to it. These ants were looking for food, because as they would stroke the caterpillar with their antennae, a drop of liquid would be coaxed out of an opening on the caterpillar's back; the ants then drank this fluid.

Leaving the moist, shady woods and returning to the world of bobolinks, buttercups, and barnyard bantams, I began thinking of our plans for the day, which included an Amish farm auction. As I entered the house, a warbling vireo was singing from the top of our big red maple, gently reminding me that some species of birds prefer the large shade trees in our lawns and parks.

Branch

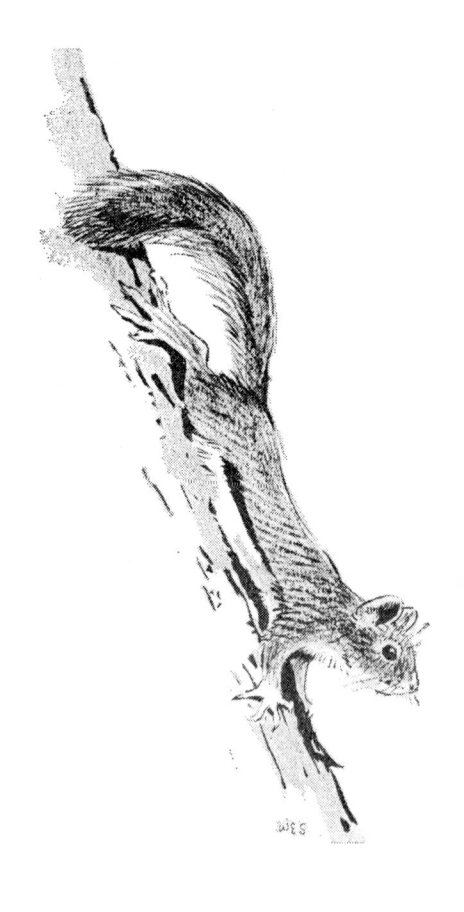

Red squirrel

LETTER FIFTEEN: *Fall 1973*

AUTUMN HERE AT SAWDUST means darkened tree trunks rising among carelessly piled carpets of golden leaves or it could be the stiff-legged and clumsy yellow jackets biting into the last few purple grapes hanging on the vines. It is limp, mildewy goldenrod leaves and bent, jaundiced cattail blades. It may be a lone, hoarse-sounding katydid or the distant roar of hundreds of blackbirds as they settle down back in the woods. Autumn gives us eerie winds and sounds, and many days of rain filling the ponds and pools. It brings gray and white swirls of juncos and flocks of lisping kinglets or a hermit thrush to be watched as it feeds on the scarlet, oval, shining drupes of a spicebush. It is a time of migrating monarch butterflies, handsome rings of brilliant yellow fly amanita mushrooms, corpulent woodchucks and raccoons, and high dayflower-blue skies.

And some years there is a very special autumn night when stars seem to glow on the ground. This uncanny phenomenon, commonly called fox fire, can be observed on a dark night following the fall cutting of our woodland trails. Apparently, the brush cutter knocks the decaying logs apart and for a few hours the exposed pieces and flakes of wood that contain the fox fire will emit a ghostly light as they lie on the ground in the darkness. I love to crumble a piece of the wood and watch the tiny luminescent shreds sift through my fingers . . . like so much fanciful star dust. Though it seems as if it should feel warm, it is not. Beneath light, the wood looks no different from any other piece of decayed wood. Like many of our discoveries at Sawdust, the finding of fox fire was accidental. Following a day of cutting the trails with his tractor, Dick had gone at dusk to see if animals were coming at night to a small pool in a side ravine. Ever the photographer, he had spotted a perfect background there of layered sandstone. However, all of this was of no avail and, as he made his way back, the batteries of his flashlight gave out. As his eyes became accustomed to the dark, he saw the first fox fire.

As we walk the fox fire trail, we usually hear one of the long-horned grasshoppers singing from a spot low to the ground;

it is a Davis's shield-bearer *(Atlanticus davisi)*. This short-winged, nocturnal species frequents thickets and woodland edges but it is difficult to observe, except when the male is singing. The role of this species in nature is not too well understood, but in captivity it is somewhat carnivorous, eating other grasshoppers. Dick will vouch for its strong jaws, I am certain, since I have seen his hand bleeding from the bite of one of them. Normally this species is brown but Sawdust Tract has a population which occasionally yields green individuals. This is the only known area where green *davisi* occur. This species is a midwestern one and as far as we are concerned here at Sawdust, from the standpoint of biogeography, our most important species are those which can be labeled as midwestern species.

The song of the shield-bearer (or shield-back) is a weak one and almost lost in the clamor of the orthopteran chorus. At the other extreme, the loudest part of the chorus emanates from the true katydid *(Pterophylla camellifolia)*. The true katydid is arboreal, and because its hind legs never harden, it is unable to fly. But the sound it produces by scraping the ridge of one wing cover across teeth on the other wing cover is a familiar one . . . katy-did, katy-did, yes, she-did. Perhaps the best time to see a true katydid is to walk in the woods the morning after the first gentle frost. As the sun begins to warm the day and crystal drops begin to patter like so much rain, you may find a true katydid attempting to crawl back up to its leafy station, from which it had tumbled during the nighttime cold.

Altogether ten species of katydid may be found on Sawdust, but the rarest of them all is the hemlock katydid *(Scudderia fasciata)*. It is one of the smallest of the katydids and lives on the hemlocks. It is so well concealed in these trees that, to collect one, you must take a sapling and beat a hemlock with it until one of the katydids is dislodged. Dr. Edward S. Thomas, curator emeritus of the Ohio State Museum, was the first to prove that the hemlock katydid can go through its entire life history while caged on a branch of hemlock.

Another crepuscular insect that is active in late summer and fall is a dragonfly named *Boyeria grafiana*. Since almost all of the dragonflies are sun-loving insects, flying only when the sun is shining brightly, this particular genus interested Dick when he read that they could be found at twilight along streams and lake shores. It occurred to him that there was a possibility that we might have some along our creek, so that evening at dusk he was sitting beside a creek pool with a very large net. Shortly, out of the gloom, a good-sized dragonfly came bouncing along. Catching it was relatively easy, since it seems to be a slow flyer. Dick brought it up to the house and because it has no common name he dubbed it the "Midnight Rambler." Upon releasing it inside, it flew around the living room walls, staying as far away from the light as possible and, surprisingly, it even flew upside down. It appeared to be extremely negative to light. Dick has since collected more of them here, one as late as ten-thirty at night. It was so dark that particular night that he could not distinguish the dragonfly itself, but a patch of sky was reflected in the creek pool and in that reflection he could see a hatch of mayflies with the dragonfly jerking through them. According to the literature, this species of *Boyeria* should be along a lake rather than a creek such as ours.

As the land about me browns and withers and wrinkles with its wintry white fringes of frost, I find myself turning to the green world of the mosses. To me they are special symbols of nature's endurance — tiny green islands, brightened by the orange, yellow, red, gray, or brown of their fruiting capsules and stalks. What is more lovely than the erect, maroon stems topped with their shaggy light gray calyptras of the moss *Pogonatum pensilvanicum (P. brevicaule),* rising an inch above a clump of bare earth? One year, very late in November, I found a species of moss I never expected to see or discover, because it is almost microscopic (one millimeter). I had brought in a soil sample from the edge of a creek trail and for some reason was examining it beneath the microscope. What I was originally searching for, I fail to recollect, but there was a specimen of *Ephemerum megalosporum* with its smooth reddish, golden sporangium looking like a miniature pumpkin nestled in a green rosette of leaves. Beneath the microscope, it was one of nature's artistic achievements, elaborately structured and perfectly designed; repeating its life cycle as unobtrusively as possible and offering only microbic competition for space on this earth. So very few people have ever seen one of these botanical gems and there would be no one to know if suddenly the species ceased to exist, yet someplace in nature this moss is important. Just as it must have a glistening drop of water to reproduce itself, something in its unseen community needs it. I wonder, what?

There are more animals this year on Sawdust than we have

ever had. Rabbits, red and fox squirrels, chipmunks, weasels, raccoons, striped skunks, opossums, woodchucks, and deer wander in and out of our yard by day and by night. Only the red fox is missing. One night a mother raccoon proceeded to tear apart one of the floor boards on our front porch and, more curious than indignant, we permitted her to continue. Very shortly she began to reach in and pull out parts of a bumblebee's nest. Of course, many angry-sounding black and yellow workers came boiling up and crawled all over her face, chest, and paws. If she was being stung, she gave no sign of it, as she calmly ate either the honey or larvae. Upon finishing her feast, she stood up to peer in our window and there were no swollen places on her face. We still are trying to solve that puzzle. The relationship between the mother raccoons and their young ones proved to be interesting; once they were weaned, they were pretty much on their own, in spite of their small size. While they still trailed behind their mothers much of the time, the mothers made no effort to protect them when danger threatened. They would run away as fast as they could, leaving the young ones there, and so it was up to the young raccoons to choose whether to follow the mother's example or not. Invariably there would be one young one in every family that failed to depart, which made it easy prey. One evening I saw a young and little raccoon, full of snarls, chasing a large skunk. The mother raccoon was watching it, too, but neither of us intervened. I have always understood that the animals in the wild cautiously avoid the skunk, but I do not believe this anymore, since time after time I have seen a skunk retreating if a raccoon becomes at all threatening. The skunk will back up, with its small head close to the ground and its tail arched high, but when the raccoon moves toward it, the skunk just turns and quickly gallops away.

Very shortly, many of these animals, singly or in family groups, will be retiring to their winter dens, and already I am beginning to wrap myself up against the cold as I go out these mornings. How I dislike seeing the fall end. Autumn may have the sadness of worn butterfly wings on some days or the crispness and sparkle of a joyful canyon creek on others, but always it is endowed with the colorfulness of a rainbow.

Maple-leaved viburnum

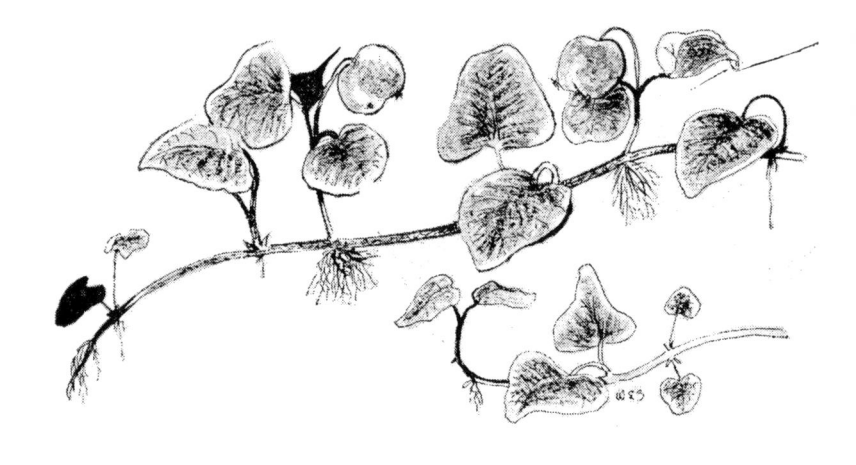

Partridge berry

Letter Sixteen: *Winter 1973*

WINTER HAS CHILLED AND BATTERED US too long, with so few days of sunshine, that I fairly jumped out of the house this morning, when I realized the wind had unexpectedly shifted during the night. The woodland stood beautiful in anticipation. I could now easily cease dreaming of what it would be like to see whales spouting their way down the Pacific coast or pansies growing in Iceland. I could forget about planning a trip to a farm in Iowa to hear the corn growing on a hot summer night or that hike into Alaska Basin in the Tetons to see the display of wild flowers therein. A harlequin duck in breeding plumage, the call of a chachalaca, a glimpse of a kit fox — all of these could wait, since suddenly the prospect of another pleasant winter walk around Sawdust seemed very precious.

A large flock of evening grosbeaks noisily and speedily passed overhead. It seems to me these wintering guests from the north are learning more and more about the sun-flowered feeding trays and are visiting Ohio in greater numbers with each passing year. I heartily agreed with Deborah, though, when she remarked, "I rather enjoy watching them at our feeder, they are such colorful and fistic birds."

Inverted long-stemmed ice goblets were suspended from the tree roots and rocky ledges just above the rushing water of the creek, while chunks of ice were being spun around in the pools. Three black Mecoptera *(Boreus brumalis)* were crouching motionless on a snowy bank, looking much like very small grasshopper nymphs ready to jump. These tiny (four to five millimeters) scorpion flies are virtually wingless, but have the curious long face which is typical of this primitive order. Their mouth is located at the end of an elongated beaklike structure. Because they are seen in the winter hopping on the snow, they are called snowfleas in the family Boreidae found here in the east, but it is brown.

Tracks of the white-footed mouse were all about and I was interested in the distance a single mouse would travel at this time of the year, some two hundred and fifty feet. They all appeared to complete their journeys safely, which was surprising considering the number of predators that were also obviously about in the woods last night.

I stopped to examine a nest of last summer's red-eyed vireo and discovered it to be half full of round wild cherry pits. In my mind's eye, I could visualize a petite mouse nestled down in that snug little swinging cradle, gnawing on the pits it had so carefully stashed away.

Although it is February, there are numerous berries remaining on the different plants and vines. The bristly greenbriers' dark berries are still firm, round, and smooth but those of the carrion-flower are a soft and wrinkled bluish mess. I pulled one of the latter apart and was startled to find a glowing ruby red large single seed in it. And nothing seems to feast eagerly on the scarlet partridgeberry. One winter I carefully counted the number of berries in a large patch of this plant, and then watched it for months. The berries remained intact, until they finally fell off; some persisted until the plants were blooming again in the summer.

There are many dead elm trees, with their loosened pieces of bark, lining the trail, and growing on some of them were bright orange reddish tufts of mushrooms (*Collybia valutipes*). The rounded caps of the mushrooms were smooth and viscid, but the stems were like brown velvet. I simply admired them, but the many old puffballs attached to the rotting stumps were given a whack, just so I could see their small clouds of spores escape.

Writing of mushroom spores reminds me of a find last December 11th. Our woodland is dotted with many ferns; in fact we have recorded twenty-nine species growing here on Sawdust, but very rarely have I ever seen the beginning of a fern plant under natural conditions. Probably every introductory biology textbook illustrates the life cycle of a fern plant, since it is an example of alternation of generations — sexual and asexual. The asexual or sporophytic generation is the familiar fern plant, but when the spores from the fern frond blow or fall on the right spot at the right time, they will produce a small, flat growth called the prothallus, which contains male and female cells. These cells develop on the underside of the prothallus, and, after being fertilized, create a new fern plant. When I discovered a light green heap of these very little heart-shaped prothallia (each less than five millimeters) growing on the side of a rooting log, I was quite excited, since it was a perfect "living" textbook illustration.

There was not much to see in the way of birdlife as I walked, although I did watch a red-bellied woodpecker pounding on something it had wedged between two limbs. Gretta likens the cap and hind neck of this woodpecker to red satin! Abruptly, the peace was shattered by loud, raucous screeches and cries. I could not imagine what I was hearing, but as I moved forward, I could see two fox squirrels high in a sugar maple. At the same time, I noticed three more of these large squirrels approaching the sugar maple, where they attempted to reach the top, too. But one of the original two squirrels there would not allow any of the others to climb up. Such vicious and noisy fighting and jerking of tails! Eventually the three squirrels gave up trying and ran away and, a little later, the two remaining squirrels mated high on a limb.

While passing a stand of planted white pines, I decided to check the trees for old nests. This particular cluster of pine trees holds a special place in my heart, because almost twenty years ago, we gave Rick (then eight years old) a bucket of pine seedlings and told him he could plant them anywhere he wished. So he trudged far up the valley and planted them in an open spot overlooking the creek. The only problem was that he became either bored or tired or careless, because he placed two seedlings together in some of the holes. Consequently there are now a few big double trees competing for space, but we hate to cut any of them down.

As I walked home, a white mist began to rise above the white snow — it was a lovely thing to see and in which to be walking. A flock of tree sparrows was splashing and dipping among pieces of floating ice in the creek and, from their twinkling chatter, I could only guess they were enjoying it.

When I returned to the house, Dick told me there was a fox lying in the orchard and that three dogs had just caught up with it and killed it. We walked over to examine it and as we bent over, the fox suddenly jumped to its feet and ran away, leaving two very astounded people behind. After eating a sandwich, I elected to follow the tracks of the fox. I found that it had left the orchard and run steadily for half a mile, until it crossed the creek and curled up beneath an old hemlock tree. It must have seen me coming, since it left there and went up over the ravine hillside. And that was where it remained until I almost walked over it. It was looking at me with such a hopeless and helpless expression that I quietly left. Regret was mixed with admiration as I retraced my steps homeward.

Katydids

Male cricket

LETTER SEVENTEEN: *Fall 1974*

CAREFULLY STEPPING OVER the four-leaf clover path flourishing near the back door, I turned and headed down our long driveway to check the mailbox. The sky was the deepest of blues with gratifying pure-white islands of clouds suspended high above. Hordes of red-legged grasshoppers bombarded my feet and legs as I moved along the sun-warmed drive. Here and there, ants were clustered about a car-flattened body of a grasshopper or black field cricket, while the squashed fallen pears had their share of feasting yellow jackets. Far lovelier to watch was a ruby-crowned kinglet restlessly searching for food among the yellow network of witch hazel blossoms, while below, dusty spindrifts arose as a song sparrow ruffled its feathers in the dried-out basin of a mud puddle. Similarly, several rabbits were rotating and rubbing their bodies along the powdery roadbed. The rabbits appeared unwilling to leave, so that I could almost have scooped them up, if I had wished.

What a year 1974 has been for rabbits, greater numbers of them here on Sawdust than ever before! Late yesterday afternoon, I watched a barred owl drop down after one out in the yard, but it missed as the rabbit vaulted to safety beneath a shed. Sweeping back up, the owl perched on a nearby branch, acting as if it didn't want the rabbit anyway. Almost immediately, the owl was the center of attention as some chickadees and titmice discovered it and as they chitter-chattered away, the owl preened and shook itself, indifferent to them. While the past season seemed to be ideal for rabbits, it was near disaster for most species of butterflies and moths on this place; what is more, no black-billed cuckoos were seen or heard, nor upland plovers and very, very few female towhees. To be specific, I saw only one. The male towhees returned, but the females just did not ever arrive.

The daily trek to retrieve the mail is never dull, although one day it must have been nearly that since I counted the steps it took to reach the box down at the end of the road, four hundred and eighty-three of them. I seldom mind if I have to await the mailman's car, since the roadside is interesting, too. In the spring and fall, the trees on its edge are often filled with migrating birds; rarely do I leave my binoculars sitting on the dining room table at home. Furthermore, it is difficult to understand that, with the many acres that comprise Sawdust, we still must go to our roadside ditches to find certain species of plants and insects, even a fish — the mud minnow.

On the shaded side of the road, across from the mailbox, the sprawling plants of the common or lesser stichwort compete for growing space along the ditch. Probably no one would notice this blossoming plant from a car as they bounced along in early summer on the rough road, but if they did, it might grieve them to see the mud flying into the faces of the chaste white and perfect star-like flowers. Such dainty little gems, with their deeply cleft petals, and, to my thinking, so poorly named, unless it is true that the plant was once used as relief for sudden, sharp pains in a person's side. I prefer the Latin name for it: *Stellaria graminea*. On the opposite side of the road, as the botanical show begins to wane with conclusion of summer, two more species appear, to grace the ditches with their white spikes of blooms; the whorled milkwort and nodding ladies'-tresses. To my delight, the ladies'-tresses *(Spiranthes cernus)* literally line the roadside here. And who wouldn't be pleased to have such a fine stand of these small orchids, with their pearly white flowers spiraling up the stalk? Since the township sends a man periodically to cut and scrape our road, I think each autumn that the orchids will be a thing of beauty gone forever, but somehow they have survived and, in fact, increased with the passing years. The road man, with his cutting bar, did destroy something one fall and we still find ourselves lamenting that afternoon. Great masses of turtlehead grow along the road, particularly where it is wet and shady. Since the Baltimore butterfly lays its eggs principally on that plant species, we always watch for the butterfly larvae in their cobwebby communal nests in the turtlehead leafage. And at last, we found some, many of them. Because this exquisite butterfly is extremely local, usually occurring only where the food plant (turtlehead) grows, we were grateful for an opportunity to follow its unusual life cycle. Knowing that the road man might suddenly appear to slice the weeds along the road, we dug three turtlehead plants with the larval webs and planted them in a marshy place near the house, leaving perhaps a dozen undisturbed along the ditch, in hopes that they would survive. They didn't — the very next day every plant was severed. Meanwhile, the plants we had moved grew and the Baltimore larvae thrived until the caterpillars went into hibernation for the winter in the webs. But then one day late in October, I woefully watched a chickadee carefully picking out the inert larvae. We should have screened them. The Baltimore butterfly is about two inches wide; its wings are black with white spots and edged with striking brick red to deep orange spots. Like the Baltimore oriole, it is named after Lord Baltimore, whose family coat-of-arms was black and orange.

Since I knew Dick was anxious to read his mail, I rather hurried back home, but not before I took time to sniff the ladies'-tresses, trying once more to detect the odor of vanilla, which some people contend the orchid possesses. Beside one of the plants, a lone scarlet-veined maple leaf was resting on a pile of dry, saffron grasses, going the way of oblivion together. I couldn't help but think of what an eighty-seven-year-old patient of Milcey's once said to her, "Time wears away, like everything else."

Later in the day, I went out to our pond to listen for mole crickets. Their song, if one can call it that, is a succession of low pitched ventriloquial notes — whirr-whirr-whirr. I always have to listen carefully, to make certain I am not confusing it with the higher-pitched notes of a snowy tree cricket. To locate a mole cricket is one of the games that interested naturalists play. Usually it sings from the entrance of its ground burrow and the minute a heavy-footed person approaches, it will crawl farther back into its tunnel. One may spend hours attempting to collect or see this curious species of the cricket family, but it is so interesting that it is worth it. They are flattened, an inch long when adult, velvety brown due to a covering of very short hair, and the front tibiae are greatly enlarged, closely resembling the forefeet of the common mole. Like the mole, they spend most of their life beneath the ground, digging tunnels and searching for food, such as plant roots, grubs, and earthworms. We have never found their eggs, which are believed to be laid in masses in a side chamber of their burrow, but Dick did find immature mole crickets swimming in the water close to our pond dam. They were the first immature specimens ever collected in the state of Ohio. It supposedly takes three years for them to reach maturity. We have found more short-winged adults than those with long wings. Occasionally, a long-winged specimen may appear around an outdoor night light. The antennae are short and the eyes tiny, as is the case in so many forms living underground. I shall never forget one torrid autumn afternoon when Dick and I were trying to acquire one of these crickets. Dick was on his hands and knees, tugging at a thick clump of grass in the wet mud, when unexpectedly I saw him scramble up and begin running as fast as he possibly could away from the spot — far away. Because I had never known him to run from anything ever before, I was surely puzzled. However, upon hearing his version, I understood. Beside the clump of grass was a large rock and nestled between the two was a nest of dried grasses, teeming with bumblebees, which he unknowingly disturbed. They had attacked immediately, in defense of their nest. He was not stung, although the bees followed and circled him for a hundred yards.

The mole crickets are in the order Orthoptera and the family Gryllidae and are found living in wet swales, along the margins of small creeks and ponds. It forever fascinates me to see two forms from different classes, resembling one another, due to adaptations or modifications of their structures for their environment or way of life. Both the mole and the mole cricket have developed spade-like front legs, with which to dig. Another example of this is a small (ten millimeters) insect, which is aptly named the toad bug. When you see them sitting or hopping along a creek or pond edge, you might think at first they were newly transformed young toads. Originally I came across these pygmy toad bugs along a creek in the hills of southern Ohio and I could never dismiss their appeal. In fact, I kept after Dick to drive us back there, so I might see them once again. But last summer, while attending a Geauga County farm auction on July 28th, I wandered over to the farmer's pond to identify the tiny dragonflies that were speeding about the edge. The dragonflies proved to be the Lilliputians of the true dragonflies around here — lovely amberwings, of the species *Perithemis tenera*. Suddenly, however, while at the pond, something hopped next to my foot. Forgetting entirely the auction with its large number of spectators, I stooped down, intent on finding out what had hopped. So perfectly did it blend in with the dirt and pebbles, I could not see anything until I moved my hand directly over the area and startled the small thing into a few more jumps. A toad bug, with its protruding oval eyes and squat form! Frantically I looked around for something to put it in, since I just had to take it home for further study, and I wanted so to have Dick photograph it. Nothing was handy, so I gently covered it with a flat rock, hoping it would remain there until I came back with a jar. Running to our truck, I retrieved a small pressed-glass compote I had bid on. Fortunately, the insect was still there when I returned. An hour earlier, I had been so pleased with my old glass compote, with a quail forming the lid's handle, but it was nothing compared to what now rested inside the jar. Once home, I tried to keep it alive, by feeding it small insects, but it died within two days. The toad bugs are in the order Hemiptera and in the family Gelastocoridae.

As I daily walk with the seasons, up and down our driveway, I cannot help but realize how different my Sawdust timetable is. For me, spring begins with the first whistling cardinal in late January and summer can come in May. Autumn always seems close by when the showy clumps of early goldenrod *(Solidago juncea)* appear in the second week of July, with their deep yellow, one-sided blossoming branches, while perched on the telephone wires stretching above these plants may be a solid line of barn swallows, already gathering for their southward journey. How graceful those birds are, as they drop from the wires and encircle the field. I think of them as the sweeping second-hand on nature's timepiece. I watch the flower buds on the fruit trees swell until their white petals open, briefly crowding one another until the dark branches are no longer visible. I know that the tiny green fruits which follow will darken into a rich ripeness. Frog and bird songs finally give way to those of the crickets and grasshoppers. A colorful succession of flowers lines the driveway, from the vivid hawkweeds to daisies and buttercups, Queen-Anne's lace, and the blue chicory to the finale of masses of purple New England asters, white wreath asters, and goldenrods with a background of fiery sumac and maple trees. Furthermore, beauty doesn't end with the coming of the wintertime, because the stiffened heads of the field flowers become fanciful etchings as they ride above unblemished piles of snow, and a frost-sparkled orchard matches the glow of last summer's fireflies there. The seasons do tumble by, however, much too quickly, and I would prolong each one, if I were able. With such reluctance I see them fade and blend into the past, though I know that next year, with Faith, I shall have another chance to view it all again. For me, there is always a bluebird softly warbling in the distance.

Katydid and beaver

LETTER EIGHTEEN: *Winter 1974*

INCHES OF SNOW HAD FALLEN last night and, always enchanted by the prospect of unbroken snowy trails, I left early for one of those vagrant walks, not seeking much other than the beautiful. There was no sunshine, but ample time.

As I passed the garden, I was glad for the snow, because only parts of last summer's weeds were showing and I did not have to feel guilty that I chose to walk rather than weed. Gardening is a curious affair here, since if a plant of whose identity I am uncertain suddenly volunteers, it is permitted to grow between the vegetables and flowers until I can tell what it is. This past summer I counted seventy-four different weed species there, from the creeping carpetweed to quaking aspen. It amuses me that the very worst transgressors are named after barnyard animals: pigweed, chickweed, henbit, goosefoot, lamb's-quarter, sow thistle. Last season's tall spreading stalks of the velvet-leaf still topped the snow there, with their attractive brown-seeded heads. While it is now considered a troublesome weed by many, at one time this annual was carefully cultivated in gardens, following its importation from India. It is a wonderful plant as far as we are concerned, not so much because of its deep yellow blossoms, but for its velvety, large heart-shaped leaves. If you have ever rubbed the soft nose of a horse, you will understand how the leaves feel to touch. And the seed heads, with their circle of firm and enduring beaked carpels, are most unusual in any dried winter arrangement. While velvet-leaf is the name given in most flower books, it also used to be called pie-marker or butter-print, and I strongly suspect that it was for this use that its seeds were saved and passed along to family and neighbors for planting. I have no idea who the first ingenious cook was to think of using the seed head for decorating her pie crusts or butter, but I can well imagine her surprised delight when she saw how perfectly it worked, to say nothing of the praise that must have been forthcoming when she took her artistic pie to the next church social or fair — no other cook could have matched that intricate aster-like print designed by nature. She must have shared her secret though, for gradually the name of velvet-leaf was changed locally to reflect that use. It belongs to the Mallow family and is technically designated *Abutilon Theophrasti,* for the early Greek scientist Theophrastus, who was successor to Aristotle as head of the Peripatetic School.

When I reached it, the woodland was as noiseless and white as a thick Ashtabula snowstorm could make it. The stumps all supported queer-looking alabastrine busts, so that at times I had the feeling that I was walking through a hall of fame of Neanderthal people. It seemed no birds nor squirrels dared to disturb them, and I, too, walked quickly by. The woods was theirs for awhile.

Down in the floodplain, clumps of small brown puffballs, still clinging to a high old rotting tree stub, attracted me. Wondering if a cloud of spores would escape even though the wood and everything about was snowy yet, I knocked one of the top-shaped puffballs with the tip of my walking stick. Sure enough, dustlike olive green spores arose from the tiny opening on top of the puffball, reminding me of a smoldering volcano. The outer layers of a puffball must be fairly resistant to moisture and its vent must remain tightly closed, or else the spores themselves are waterproof. The Indians are supposed to have used the spores of puffballs to stop a nosebleed or a bleeding wound.

I easily crossed the frozen creek, passing at one point a huge boulder left there by the last glacier. It is well over five feet in diameter and it often makes me think of Professor Agassiz, who used to travel about our country before the Civil War delivering lectures on his theory of continental glaciation. The professor must have had a voice like a bull because at times he would speak to a crowd of five thousand. Most of Sawdust is flat because of continental glaciation.

Fortunately, the continental glaciers are a thing of the past, although someday they may return. But nature can still be violent without having the violence occurring on such a vast scale. Some winters our creek pools freeze solidly and then, with the rains, the ice is lifted out in enormous blocks a foot thick, eight to ten feet wide, and as much as ten to fifteen feet long. Windows of ice will pile up along the floodplain trail as high as six feet. As they melt and move about, everything is ground to bits and the earth left bare. Just beyond the large boulder, the remains of a big black cherry tree stood in silent testimony to one of last summer's violent electrical storms. Lightning hit the tree and it must have literally exploded, since toothpicks the size of two-by-fours, eight to ten feet long, were sticking yet in the ground at crazy angles above the snow. And I still remember the cedar waxwing we found dead on its nest, hit by a large hailstone, or the nestling orioles tossed to their death by a wild windy storm last June.

On I trudged, though, up the valley; a peaceful valley at that time, but overhead the sky had begun to darken. And before I climbed up to Tupelo Hill, the snow was coming down, noiselessly at first, but then with the heavy crystal sound of snowfall without wind. The snow was deeper there and it seemed a long way across the open hilltop, until I heard robins. As many as ten of them were feeding on the oval bluish tupelo berries. The tupelo blossoms had furnished quite a honey flow last summer and now the birds were benefitting from both the bees and the trees. I just cannot think of a single thing in the natural world that isn't dependent on something else to maintain life, unless there is a tiny bacterium that is able to exist only on inorganic material.

But the bird for the morning, I almost missed. As black and gray and white as the landscape itself, a northern shrike was poised there in a hickory tree, with its horizontally held tail catching the snowflakes. It was only the second one I have ever observed on Sawdust. The other one was seen trying to seize a tufted titmouse at our bird feeder. Memories always have a way of returning, and the shrike recycled one. It was a gusty, cold April day in 1931 and I was walking the mile to school, taking the short cut that led me past an orchard, through fields and a small woodlot. As I think about it, it was a marvel that I ever arrived at school in time because there were so many new birds and plants for me to see. But on that particular occasion I heard a disconnected song, with soft trills, gurgles, and pipings. It was coming from a bird perched on the woven wire fence next to me, singing even though it was having difficulty maintaining its position in the wind. But the spurts of song, the ruffled gray feathers, were my introduction to a shrike. And strangely enough, it was the only time in my life that I have ever heard a shrike sing.

I watched the birds for awhile and I looked some hawthorne trees over along the trail to see if by any chance the shrike had fastened a bird or mouse to one of their thorns, but if it did I failed to find it.

With still half a mile to cover, I moved on. The secret to all life appeared to be buried so much deeper when a snowstorm masked the earthen maze below it. That nothing, save identity, is ever lost in the natural world is harder to believe at such a time. I missed the reassuring green trailing stems of the partridge berry with its ruby-like fruit, a shiny black beetle running over brittle leaves, or a delicate petal shifting with the wind. But as I neared our farmyard, the sound of the roosters crowing reached out through the dense snowfall with a special message all its own.

Northern shrike

Beaver

Letter Nineteen: *Spring 1975*

A SOFT MAY RAIN was gently falling as I wandered for hours this morning — through our woodland, along the length of the rich floodplain, across the cutover, out in the more open abandoned pasture now dotted with hawthornes, viburnums, tupelos, witch hazels, red maples, and many others, until at last I crossed the field adjacent to the house. Everywhere the songs of the birds, blending with the rain sound, seemed to be sweeter than ever before, as though each drop of water had captured a bit of lyric, not releasing it until the rain drop rolled down a colored petal or leaf and splattered apart on the earth. The floodplain was a green corridor with masses of golden ragwort rising above spotless blossoms of the Canada violet, and the delicate flowering panicles of one of the bluegrasses *(Poa alsodes)* were graceful despite their burden of glistening raindrops. Briefly two intrepid red efts shared my walk, such bright spots of color as they crawled over the dark ground of the trail. I would expect them to be seen promptly and devoured by something, but supposedly their skin glands secrete a toxic substance that is somewhat irritating to the mouths of predators. The red eft is a land stage, which may last up to three years, of the aquatic red-spotted newt. In some places, however, the eft form or land stage is omitted and the spotted newts never leave the water, transforming directly from the larval stage to the aquatic adult. While newts look like other salamanders, they are in a separate family. Many children could tell you one of the most obvious distinctions between the two; a salamander is slimy to the touch, but a newt is not.

A month ago the scent of the sweet-tipped pendulous blooms of the sugar maple trees permeated the air, but today only the redolence of warm, moist soil and the unrestrained green sprouting organisms was notable.

As I lingered a while by one of my special pools along Penny Creek where the venerable hemlocks are beginning to lean, a trio of thrushes began to sing — a wood thrush, a Swainson's thrush, and a veery. Their hauntingly beautiful madrigals flowed out, up and down the scale, blending into one of the finest woodland recitals I may ever be privileged to hear. Thoreau, perhaps, heard something similar when he wrote, "Music is the sound of the circulation in nature's veins. It is the flux which melts nature." Wood thrushes and veerys are summer residents here, but the Swainson's thrush will be gone shortly on its way to the vast northern spruce-fir forests.

At one point along the floodplain trail, I took time to detour up a side valley where the ground is usually wet and the leaf mold deep and rich. Goldie's fern and the narrow-leaved spleenwort thrive there, but what I was actually searching for was a green dragon. Sharing the genus Arisaema with the jack-in-the-pulpit, this unusual plant, with its long and slender spadix, is noteworthy. Years ago, we planted a green dragon there and it reappeared each spring but never reproduced itself. Last year it was missing and there was no trace of it this morning either. Our policy through the years here at Sawdust has been not to introduce any plants but we did make an exception with the curious green dragon.

I watched as a blue jay imitated the two-syllabled scream of the red-shouldered hawk; with its black bill closed it pumped out its chest and bobbed forward with each "kee-way." The jays are very good at this but one bird that certainly amazes me is a starling, which sits high up in our red maple, imitating an upland plover. I must admit, as I walk across the yard, I enjoy hearing that captivating, resounding whistle, even though I know it is an imposture. A perching Wilson snipe surprised me with its loud call, which was reminiscent of the cries of both the flicker and the guinea hen. When I described it to Dick, he said that one time he and Dr. Oberholser were birding near Fern Lake in Geauga County and they had heard the same call, emanating from a snipe poised on a fence post. Dr. Oberholser commented that he had never heard that particular cry before.

Somehow, as the resounding bird chorus mounts each morning, I am left with the warm feeling that our natural world here is still holding its own against the buffeting that is so constantly being discussed these days. It is a reassuring and pleasant boost for each new day. Scientists have spent much time proving that birds do not sing out of happiness; I surmise the professors are fearful that some of us might be misled in our interpretation of what is one of life's brighter bonuses. And while I must agree with their findings to some extent, when I observe a parent wren alternately scolding and singing as it watches a black snake coiling around and entering its nesting cavity, I still believe that the birds enjoy and attempt to perfect their melodies, with no inner agony to trouble their spirit. A sick rooster rarely crows. Poor Ph. D.'s — of the two, I think the singing birds appear happier.

For approximately the last two decades, beaver have been reappearing and establishing themselves around our county of Ashtabula. We have watched this with much interest and everytime we would find one working along Penny Creek, we hoped so much that they would remain, but the hard layered sandstone and shale creek bottom here apparently discourage them and they would move on. However, early this month one found our barnyard pond. The muskrat bank-burrow was taken over, aspen trees soon began to topple, and the leak in the dam was reduced to a trickle. As eager as we were for the opportunity to study a beaver, we had to restrain ourselves at first, lest we frighten it away. Very few doors were slammed, no nails were pounded, and we practically tiptoed about the yard. We had to content ourselves, just knowing that at last we had a resident beaver; we didn't even know if we had a wandering two-year-old or a pair of beaver. But for the last two weeks, we have been going over to the pond in the later afternoon to watch. There is only one very big beaver and we have dubbed her "Big Fat Mama" because she is either expecting young or has just given birth to them — we cannot tell which. Each evening at about the same time, she will climb out of the water, settle herself back on her haunches, and then proceed to rub and massage her extended belly and whitish mammae. With her eyes closed and her head tipped back, she makes quite a comical picture as she does this. After several minutes of that, she then gets down to the serious business of grooming her dark fur; with her long white claws, she combs each leg, behind her ears, her head and back, and finally even her scaly, spatulate tail is cleaned (by mouth). Though I cannot see it through my binoculars, her webbed hind feet have double or split second claws, which aid her in this grooming. Never has she worked on repairing the dam while we have been there, but in the short time that she has been with us, we find it incredible how she has fixed the dam leak. For years the pond has never retained its full capacity of water. Though Dick had wheeled countless loads of clay to the gap in the dam and mixed it with branches beaver-style and even though at one point we brought in a bulldozer for two days, we never succeeded in plugging the leak the way Big Fat Mama has. We think she is a much more proficient engineer than lumberjack, however.

While she has very little difficulty in felling a tree, it seldom lands in the water. If the tree gets hung up or if she does not drag it into the water within several days, Dick takes the chain saw and cuts up the tree and throws it into the pond. A tree is worthless to her as food if she cannot get it into the water within a week. The very big aspens she cuts into until they are almost ready to fall, and then she lets the wind bring them down. When a whole tree falls into the water, she will eat entirely many of the smaller branches and twigs, like so much celery, shoving them into her mouth with her front paws as she balances her body in the water. The larger limbs will be cut off, the bark eaten, and the next morning the pond will have many of these peeled pieces of wood floating about, while others are piled on the ground over her burrow in the bank, which is, of course, under water. How subtly she swims across the pond with no visible effort on her part. Occasionally she will drift over and look up at me with her small black eyes. I wonder if her curiosity matches mine.

This evening as usual I went and sat down beside the pond rather envying Big Fat Mama being able to swim about in it. She pays very little, if any, attention to the other forms of life that come and go. A phoebe, hitting the water as it dipped down after an insect, seemed of interest only to me. I have yet to see, though, what she does when one of the pond's snapping turtles surfaces. A green heron flew in, landing on a jumble of willow branches. Slowly lifting one bright orange foot and then the other one, it moved along a branch peering down into the water but the swift downward flicking of its tail destroyed any illusion of calmness on the part of the heron. I remained there long after I could no longer distinguish much in the warm and misty nighttime darkness. The deep, gusty-throated rolling sounds of the bullfrogs arose, sometimes singly, sometimes in unison, from all sides of the pond, punctuated by the abrupt "glubs" of the green frogs. I thought how the frogs would benefit with the arrival of the beaver and then I began to wonder how much of the land surrounding the pond will eventually be flooded. Will the sprawling wild rose bush be inundated, or the massive clumps of swamp milkweed and cardinal flower? And then there is the Scotch pine that Carl Hamann added one spring day many years ago, and our beloved Lisa's grave, placed near where she used to wade into the pond on a hot day. Slowly I came to realize how nature replaces and replenishes as it displaces. Just as I reluctantly stood up to leave, a torrent of song burst forth from the woods on the opposite side of the pond. Though I could not see the singer, I knew it was an ovenbird. Perhaps it, too, was loathe to have this day of melodies in late May come to an end.

White-footed mouse

Letter Twenty: *Summer 1975*

THE NIGHT HAD BEEN HOT and so was the morning. No air moved to cause even a single aspen leaf to tremble or twirl, nor were there any quick-silvery dew drops resting lightly on the pale green leaves of the yellow touch-me-nots as I crossed, dry-shod, the ravine runlet behind the barn. All was hushed. The whole world of Sawdust seemed to have stopped singing. The early sun, poised in the sky to my right, reminded me of a big red poppy — a flamboyant, hussy-like poppy. For days those solar rays had been heating the air and searing the soil until long cracks began to appear on the forest floor and our Penny Creek was reduced to doomed pools of ebbing life.

Only once before could I recall such a siege of heat and dryness here — and never so early in the summer. Even the trees appeared to have switched off their air-conditioning units. The woodland was barely cooler than the farmland I had just left. At least, no worrisome mosquitoes hummed around my face and hands as I wandered through the heavy-heated silence. This day my walk was more of a laboratory exercise than were my usual joyful aesthetic searches. Here was an interesting world of thrips, spiders, aphids and ants, damselflies, scavenger beetles, robber and scorpion flies, wasps, bees, and butterflies — all spiritedly responding to the sunshine, while the crayfish were digging deeper and deeper into creek banks.

I could see belated blooming daisies in the clearing with more than their usual share of thin dark thrips siding their way among the white petals, now and then pausing to threaten one another by raising the tip of an abdomen. Well, that's not truly accurate, since I don't know if the posturing looks as bellicose to a thrip as it does to me. Maybe it is just their way of saying "howdy." I don't even know if they are able to see one another. In fact, one day I realized how little I knew about these insects, although all my life I had been shaking the tiny black critters off daisy bouquets. (I did know that the time to pick a bunch of daisies was right after a heavy cloudburst; a good hard rain is a fine natural insecticide.) At any rate, I commenced looking up all I could find about thrips, only to conclude that nobody else bothered very much with them either. They suck on the plant juices with an asymmetrical beak; have four fringed wings, when wings are present; their antennae are short, with six to nine segments; most thrips are only two millimeters long, the largest is five millimeters. Male thrips are scarce and the females mostly reproduce by parthenogenesis.

Thrips are widespread in their geographic distribution with nearly six hundred species in North America. There is a bright scarlet species that feeds on fungi and another one that feeds on the flowers of the Jack-in-the-pulpit. I shall search for those two; and while I must admit finding an Indian arrowhead would be far more exciting, I do hope I am successful. I could commend their order, Thysanoptera, to that new breed of young scientists who are all well armed with grants and computers as they march into the fields and laboratories; for, as Eugene Odum stated in his *Fundamentals of Ecology,* there are about one and a half million thrips to be found per acre. Perhaps I should also mention here for those extremely ambitious modern biologists that there are eighty-nine million six hundred and three thousand mites per acre!

As I followed the shaded trail up the big valley, I found a delightful botanical crowd to study. The brown, withered, fertile stalks of the rattlesnake fern were tipping over, while its close relative, the leathery grape fern, was just beginning to unfurl its firm, heavy fronds. Green berries or fruit decorated the maple-leaved viburnums, May-apples, yellow mandarins, Canada Mayflowers, doll's eye, trailing strawberry, and the wild-oats, to name a few. The wild-oats' large (one and a half inches long), green, three-sided capsule looked as tempting to eat as anything in the woods, but I seldom experiment. Clustered berries on the Solomon-plume were olive green with red spatters. Some plants still just had tight flower buds, such as the wild leeks or the horsebalm (stoneroot). Other species were in full bloom, all of them white: wood-nettle, daisy-fleabane, water pimpernel, water-horehound, water-hemlock, clammy hedge-hyssop, black cohosh, and white avens. Having white petals in that jumble of greens may be reasonable, since to perpetuate the species a plant is best pollinated by some insect; and a white blossom will surely be more obvious to a passing bee or fly in such a dark and shady place. But maybe I just like to think all of nature is cunningly contrived. Oh, well . . .

Continuing on my warm way, I was glad to have the flowers to look at, since the birds were making themselves pretty scarce. I crossed the creek below Tupelo Hill, where the trumpet-weeds reached up eight feet and halberd-leaved tearthumbs clung to my slacks. The odor of peppermint suddenly saturated the air as I stepped on the leaves of the plants growing among the rocks of the creek bed. I climbed on up to the top of Tupelo Hill, trading the songs of the red-eyed vireos for the company of an indigo bunting and some field sparrows. As I moved along the trail — a grassy ribbon between the tall weeds, bushes, and shrubby trees — brown wood nymph butterflies *(Cercyonis pegala)* kept flying up just ahead of my feet. I counted thirty-one of them in just a little less than half a mile. I liked them, but I detested the buzzing deer fly that continually swung around and around my head. I didn't mind a bit leaving that fly behind when I finally entered the shady woods again.

As I walked the loop, I passed the remains of three separate sawdust piles. They are now barely distinguishable; but when we first bought this place, the piles were very high — with gigantic pokenweeds flourishing on all their exposed, rich heaps. Altogether there were nine such sawdust piles, hence the name for our farm. Much of the big ravine and the floodplain were left intact by the lumbermen, as well as ten acres here and there of big timber — plus, of course, all the fields; but about three hundred acres had been thoroughly slaughtered. And what a fantastic biological maze it proved to be! — with its endless variety of plants, animals, and insects in the jungle of fallen tree tops, blackberry bushes, and brushy saplings. We are a little wistful as we see much of all this entering into secondary forest conditions, because it means we no longer have several pairs of chestnut-sided warblers or yellow-breasted chats nesting, for example, and such things as the large eyed-elater beetles or bessy-bugs are now difficult to find.

Jared Kirtland knew about Ashtabula County and chestnut-sided warblers because in 1853 he described that warbler in a newspaper called *The Family Vision:*

> ...although this elegant Sylvia usually retires beyond the lakes to nest and pass the warmer months, it sometimes remains here in considerable numbers. For two years past I have frequently observed it during the summer in Ashtabula county in a neglected field, thickly covered with briars and shrubs ... it was full

> of life and activity, always on the alert; yet sitting silently in the dense thickets . . . I discovered after long watching, a single nest in an almost inpenetrable thicket. It was placed in the fork of a slender shrub about four or five feet from the ground. There were three eggs, together with one of the cowbirds, deposited in it . . .

While the life style of Ashtabula County residents has drastically changed since Kirtland wrote that, the chestnut-sided warbler has not. How refreshing is the continuity found in nature. Basically, I guess that I resist change unless I know it is in the natural order of things. I would like always to be able to see a red-shouldered hawk circling overhead, to hear a robin singing at twilight, or to know that a white-footed mouse is nibbling on a pit of a wild cherry somewhere out there in the darkness.

It was nine o'clock in the morning when I returned home and already the tawny orange day-lilies beside the back door were wide open. When I had left at six o'clock, their buds were just beginning to look a bit interested in the prospect of facing a brand new world. Dick asked me what I had seen and I answered, "not much." So then he told me there was a leafcutting bee working on the bittersweet vine which coils up on our front porch trellis. After a speedy glass of iced tea, I carried a chair outside to make myself comfortable while I awaited the leafcutter.

About fifteen minutes later the stocky bee arrived, and it is certainly one of nature's better shows to see her cut a green circle out of a leaf. The bee lands on the leaf and begins, chewing counter-clockwise, with specially designed flattened mandibles. It is amazing how evenly and quickly she works — taking only twenty seconds to cut out a circle of about half-an-inch in diameter. Carrying each bit of leaf away with her to her nest, she finally fastens the pieces of leaves together to form a cell in which she will deposit an egg. By noon the bee (I am only assuming it was the same bee) had made six trips to the bittersweet vine. Not all the pieces she snipped out were round: two were slightly oval and one was merely half a circle, when she chewed out a piece from the edge of the bittersweet leaf.

After lunch, I wandered over to our pond, where I made the most exciting find of the day on the wet mud along the water's edge: a spotted thyris *(Thyris maculata),* an extremely small moth. As it walked about flicking its wings as a wasp does, I didn't even recognize at first that this super-sensitive midget was a moth. It was no bigger than a deer fly, with brown and orange scalloped wings and what looked like white spots in both pairs of wings. Because of these light translucent spots, they are called window-winged moths.

There are two young beaver now swimming about our pond, with their small tails sticking straight up out of the water. Lighter in color than their mother and already the size of a small adult muskrat, they appear to be confused by their tails — not quite yet knowing how to manage them. Their mother is still carrying mouthfuls of green herbage to them in the lodge. While swimming about, they often seize a piece of wood to play with, rolling it over and over in the water, at the same time attempting to chew on the bark. The young ones are on their own as they swim around, but if the mother becomes alarmed, her tail heaves up out of water high over her head and smacks down loudly into the water as she dives. Then the young ones will usually disappear, too.

A Baltimore oriole was nesting in one of the big aspens by the pond, so Dick screened it off with heavy wire. It was fortunate he did, because, before the young orioles were fledged, all the trees around it were toppled. Three pairs of Baltimore orioles have nested within sight and hearing of our farmyard again this year, all in aspens. Quite frequently the orioles come to the bird table for suet.

As I write this, the darkness outside is softly descending to end the two hundredth day of the year. The day-lilies of this morning had almost twelve hours of perfection, but now have closed forever. Yet the fragrant blossoms of the evening-primrose and the white lychnis are beginning to open and multitudes of spiders have already spun out their gossamer nets, all awaiting insects of the evening and the night. Our swashbuckling guinea clatters into the peaceful twilight with his daily spirited valediction, delivered from his roost in the large red maple, while overhead, a few stars are beginning to show.

C & H

COLOPHON

LETTERS FROM SAWDUST has been published for
the Cleveland Museum of Natural History
by the Cobham and Hatherton Press
in an edition of one thousand copies.
The text has been set in twelve-point Granjon and the
display type in Garamond Bold by Robert M. Starkman
of the Superior Linotype Company of Cleveland.
The paper is Mohawk Superfine, Smooth Finish,
80 lb. Text, Softwhite.
It has been bound by the Forest City Bindery of Cleveland.
Twenty copies have been especially bound
by Jan Sobota of Cleveland.